FULL CIRCLE

A MEMOIR

FULL CIRCLE
FULFILLING THE PROMISE

DIANE HANSON

A Division of WINEPRESS PUBLISHING

Pleasant Word (a division of WinePress Publishing, PO Box 428, Enumclaw, WA 98022) functions only as book publisher. As such, the ultimate design, content, editorial accuracy, and views expressed or implied in this work are those of the author.

Unless otherwise noted, all scriptures are taken from the *Holy Bible, New International Version®, NIV®*. Copyright © 1973, 1978, 1984 by the International Bible Society. Used by permission of Zondervan. All rights reserved.

Scripture references marked KJV are taken from the King James Version of the Bible.

Scripture references marked NASB are taken from the New American Standard Bible, © 1960, 1963, 1968, 1971, 1972, 1973, 1975, 1977 by The Lockman Foundation. Used by permission.

ISBN 13: 978-1-4141-1271-8
ISBN 10: 1-4141-1271-8
Library of Congress Catalog Card Number: 2008906391

CONTENTS

PREFACE

LIFE IS TOUGH. Some of us are born into a life where just surviving is a daily challenge. For others, life may appear pretty good to those on the outside, but behind closed doors there is suffering. I'm sharing my story in an effort to offer hope to those who may be going through various life challenges.

We all want a break from the pain, and some people may turn to self-destructive means to find relief. The breaking point is there for all of us; it's just a matter of how far we can be pushed.

While I understand this tendency, I finally learned that the healthiest and most effective answer in getting through life's challenges is establishing a relationship with God. Throughout the difficult times I've faced in my life, I needed to learn that I couldn't handle them all myself and to turn to God for help. This book is about faith and how one goes about finding it.

Some people who experience hardship turn away from God instead of turning to him for help. This is when many people may question God and ask him, "Why?" God does not promise life will be free from heartache, but he does promise to help us through it. When you are going through a hard time, you need God more than ever. God gives you someplace to turn, and he can give you strength, direction, and peace when you seek it. Hardships can actually help us to become wiser and can build our character. The saying "What doesn't kill you only makes you stronger" has a lot of truth to it.

We all hear people talk about "turning to God," but saying and doing are two entirely different things. Faith does not feel real to a lot of people. In our society, we want evidence of everything. It makes sense to me; I've questioned my faith too. We want proof, and often we think someone who claims to have a "close and personal relationship with God" is in their own little world. I get that. I also know that Christianity can fuel a lot of mixed feelings. Unfortunately, there is a lot of hypocrisy out there that can hurt rather than help someone in his or her desire to learn more.

Often doubt holds us back from turning to God as we face challenges. How do we get from doubting God to really reaching out to him? When we doubt, we are not trusting in God 100%. It is so natural for us to be fearful or to worry, although it means we have not yet learned to turn our worries over to God. OK, I know it is not easy and you may be thinking, "*How* do I do that?" Or you may be thinking, "But I try. I just can't help it."

God wants you to reach out to him for help. Opening up your heart, mind, and soul, and being honest with God about what you are going through is important.

I hope that reading my book may be a place to start, by your learning of the personal journey I've gone through. The reason I am sharing it is to attempt to help you relate and find hope. I often felt as though I faced some of my challenges alone. Friends and family tried to help, but since they had not experienced the same challenges themselves, they could not fully understand. I am grateful that with Christ, I was never really alone.

My book deals with various life issues—from love and struggles to have children, to health challenges and near tragedy. In my efforts to praise God for what he's done for me, I vowed to do what I can by sharing my story of hope and faith with you.

I do not for a minute believe I know it all. I have learned a lot from so many people, whom I believe God has put into my life to teach me. When I seek God, I have been blessed by seeing him through others. It's difficult for me to be vulnerable and open myself up for all to see. It's frightening to me, yet I pray my words and my stories will somehow help you in your journey through life.

When you read my book, try saying a prayer to God to help the words you are reading really sink in. I hope I can help you see and experience the true meaning of achieving "peace beyond understanding." See how it goes. You will never know until you try, right?

ACKNOWLEDGMENTS

I WANT TO GIVE a heartfelt thanks to all of my wonderful friends and family who encouraged and inspired me to overcome my fears and to budget my time in order to write this book. There are so many who have made my life meaningful—from my husband, Tim, and our four little girls, to my parents, my brother, my in-laws, and our church family. I appreciate all of the support from my great friends: Jennifer, Gail, Annie, Tiffany, Kathy, Laura, Sara, Paula, Melissa, Carol, Sue, Adrienne, Minde, Lisa, Stacey, Jody, Laurie, Terri, Alicia, and Pastor Sheryl, who have brought me confidence to spread my wings.

The Tapestry

My life is but a weaving
Between my Lord and me.
I cannot choose the colors,
He worketh steadily.

Oftentimes He weaveth sorrow
And I in foolish pride,
Forget He sees the upper
And I the underside.

Not till the loom is silent
And the shuttles cease to fly,
Shall God unroll the canvas
And explain the reason why.

The dark threads are as needful
In the Weaver's skillful hand
As the threads of gold and silver
In the pattern He has planned.

—*Author Unknown*

CHAPTER 1

THE SEEDS ARE
PLANTED

WHEN I DECIDED to write a memoir, I found that it can be difficult to tie the story together, particularly when there is still a large part of my life to live. Since my memoir's main theme identifies with my faith journey, I'm going to start it off simply by saying that as a little girl, I was taught about God and Jesus. We celebrated Christian holidays through our Lutheran Church, we listened to the sermons in church (although I will admit I had a difficult time identifying with the "preachy" style of delivery back then), and the seeds were planted. I think the fact that I used to pray to God as a child may have helped, although I never really "got it." I just prayed to him like he was my invisible friend.

Growing up, my family was, in many ways, a typical "all-American" family. I mean this in the true sense in that we were not perfect. We were financially conservative—I had what I needed, but not necessarily what I thought I wanted. We shopped at Sears or JC Penney for clothes, and I considered myself lucky if I had a "Garanimals" outfit or two (Does anyone reading this remember that brand of clothes? If not, all of the outfits could mix and match), yet I also wore my brother's hand-me-down snow boots or "snowmobile suit" as we called them in the 70s.

Our relatives are all quite different, but I consider us to be close. As referenced in the hand-me-down comment, I do have one brother named Dean, who is three and a half years older than I am. He has gorgeous blue eyes, thick, dark hair, and great complexion—he takes after my father, with the exception of the hair (we both thank mom for that)—and my brother is developmentally disabled. When mom was pregnant with Dean, everything went very well until his delivery. His umbilical cord was wrapped around his neck three times. As a result, he had minor brain damage due to lack of oxygen.

He is the absolute sweetest, best brother any girl could have asked for. We looked out for each other growing up. Friends tell me that they think I am the way I am because of my relationship with my brother. Which way is that? Good question. I think it is a nice way of explaining why I didn't "get" sibling rivalry, sarcasm, or competition. It is also a way of explaining my ability to always look at things from another person's perspective.

I believe if you truly want to understand someone, you need to walk a day in the other person's shoes.

My parents are different from each other, but they are very much in love. They met in college and Mom became a Registered Nurse and Dad became a chemist. Together they taught us everything we needed. They loved us, provided for us, and were always there for us. We were never spoiled, nor were we given a pass from hard work, and we were taught the important foundations of life. I am very grateful for them.

My mother came from a rather formal family, with big Sunday dinners and parents who always dressed appropriately. For a visual, my maternal grandparents, whom I adored, were very similar in appearance to George Bush Senior and his wife, Barbara. My grandpa always had a suit on, and Grandma almost always wore a dress or pastel-colored suit. They always attended church, which was walking distance from their modest home in a small Wisconsin town.

My maternal grandparents were also my godparents. While they are now both deceased, my greatest memory is walking to church with them, while holding their hands, and skipping down the sidewalk.

My cousins, brother, and I used to spend a week or two at my grandparent's home every summer. We had a blast. It was old fashioned and what life is "supposed" to be—safe, happy, and full of Grandma's homemade cakes and cookies.

Grandma made her life what it was. She was never one to complain, although she had every right to. Her parents and several of her brothers and sisters died of TB when she was only five years old. One of her older brothers and his wife took her in. It was like a Cinderella story in many ways. The sister-in-law made my grandma sleep in the attic, on a wooden plank put across the attic beams, and only provided a small blanket to keep her warm. This was very difficult in the cold winters. The sister-in-law also beat her. Eventually, when she was still young, she ran away by stowing away on a train and going to her loving cousin's home. She was welcomed in and soon attended boarding school. Eventually she met my grandfather, who happened to be engaged to another woman at the time. Thank God he ended up breaking off the engagement (I feel for the poor lady) and married my grandma, or my story never would have started. Life is interesting, isn't it?

My grandma always made me feel loved. Once, as we walked back from Ben Franklin (where we could get many treats and tiny toys with a budget of fifty cents) with my cousins, she told me, "You are very special. You always remember that." The way she said it really made me wonder. I know everyone is special in his or her own way, but she made me feel like my unique gifts from God made me special for a certain reason. With grandma, I always felt completely understood, loved, and accepted for who I was.

In regard to my faith journey, I vividly remember a story my grandma shared with me. She was a nurse for many years. In fact, the hospital/clinic she worked at was very close to the church. She told me about a friend whom she had cared for when she was in the hospital. This friend was dying. She shared with me how she held her friend's hand as she died. Her friend actually talked to my grandma as she described her journey to heaven. I know, it's hard to believe. If it was not my own grandma, I would not have believed it either. Her friend said, "Oh, Dell (Grandma's nick name), it's so wonderful and peaceful. It is so beautiful, like the most amazing day in spring. I wish you could see it." Then the grip on my grandma's hand loosened, and her friend was gone.

This story impacted me deeply from that point forward. As a result of hearing her story, I've never been afraid to die (well, maybe a little) and will tell the story to anyone when the opportunity presents itself.

My father came from a very different background. His mother was Italian and was raised by her Italian aunt, because her own mother died during childbirth (when his mother was born). She and her brother and sister were very poor. The depression hit them hard, and I always marveled at the stories they used to tell about those tough times. Even when finances improved over the years, and during the time in which I grew up, they still saved used wrapping paper, aluminum foil, and every scrap of food. I learned to appreciate this and still do.

My dad's father was French, and he fell head over heels in love with my grandma. I always got the impression that Grandma did a great job playing "hard-to-get." But she eventually gave in and married him. While they were married, their home was extended to include Dad's Italian great aunt (who did not speak English), and for some time, his mom's sister. Dad and his sister grew up respecting the importance of protecting your finances and survival. Both of my parents knew a good education was a privilege and worth pursuing into college.

Once my parents married and had my brother and me, I guess I would describe our church life as "luke-warm." My mother was much more eager than my father to attend church. He seemed indifferent to it all. Mom wanted Dean and me to grow up in the church, and while we didn't attend every Sunday, we attended often enough that the pastor and members knew us.

My father was raised Catholic and was involved in the church as he grew up. As a young adult, however, this all changed. He had been in the army, and during target practice a stray bullet hit him in the eye. He was alone, away from family and friends, and he was scared. He asked for a priest to come and pray with him while he was in the hospital. Instead of helping my father, the priest was crass and cold. My father's level of faith changed after that day. He questioned organized faith groups, and to some extent, he turned away from the church. I knew this bothered my mother, although we just got used to Dad's non-enthusiastic interest in the church.

As I got older, I hoped this attitude would change, although I had no idea how this could be accomplished.

Despite this, my brother and I did attend Sunday school and Vacation Bible School, and we were both confirmed in our church. We were, overall, pretty decent kids, and it appeared that we were doing all right.

I admit that during my teenage years, I chose to follow my own path (as many of us do). I was more interested in what I wanted, not what God wanted. It didn't seem realistic to be a strong follower of God as a teenager. Unfortunately, I was from a very small town, and it wasn't considered "cool" to be involved in the church. I would tip-toe on the edge and was close to taking the full plunge towards God many times, but I never quite made it. My parents wanted me to go out with a wonderful young man who conducted his life responsibly and how God would want. I thought it more interesting to date someone who was a little more "dangerous" and exciting. Not overly so, just enough to tip-toe a little on the other side.

My teenage years were tough. Few people really knew me. If it wasn't for some closer friends, I don't know what I would have done. So many kids were hurtful and insecure—something I didn't deal with in my family. My brother and I never learned sarcasm or teasing. I certainly "walked by the beat of my own drum," and in many ways still do (although now I am happy with who I am). Back then, though, I couldn't wait to graduate, and I counted the days until I could be away from it all.

After college, as I matured, I started to see the light again. I would seek God's help with struggles in relationships and my career path. One of the first times God sent me a "sign" was when I had just quit my job selling for a magazine and was stressed as I was deciding what to do for another job. I had some options, one of which included selling cars. I knew it was not the right path for me. I remember going to bed one night with the Sunday paper and all of the ads for employment and saying a prayer to God to lead me down the right path.

The next morning, I woke up and rolled to a sitting position. Sleepily I looked down on the floor and sighed as I glanced at the paper. It had been opened to a page under a different section of employment, one that was not quite the right match. A particular ad seemed to jump off the page. It was for an "Advertising Coordinator" position. It was more administrative than what I had done in the past, but it was as if God was telling me, "This is where you must go!"

There was no doubt in my mind that I was being led to work at this company, and I had absolutely no reason why. I just had to trust. Yes, it sounds pretty crazy.

People may wonder how I knew this was really "God" leading me versus a gut instinct. There is no concrete evidence, of course. If there were, I wouldn't need to write this book. I just knew. I was also grateful for the concrete discernment of this realization, because I know it's hard to achieve.

The industry this position was in is the opposite of something someone like me would ever consider, but I knew I could not object. When meeting with the Human Resources director, I knew I couldn't tell him the *real* reason I was applying for the job. Since I was overqualified, I had to convince him why I wanted it. Can you imagine if I did share the real reason? I can see it now. He would have looked at me with his eyebrows raised, a smile on his face, and mumbled something like, "OK, ah, that sounds great! Tell you what, I do have some other applicants I have to interview, but when we are ready, we'll let you know!"

I *did*, however, convince the HR director that I was looking for a non-commission job with lower stress and a regular paycheck. I got the job, and the story continues.

Little did I know God's intentions.

CHAPTER 2

MY ANGEL ON EARTH

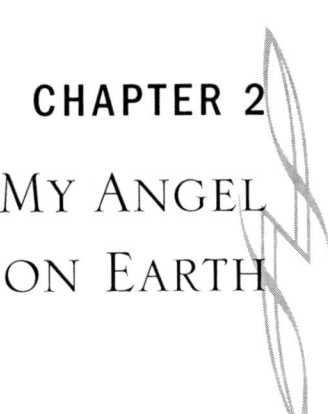

WHILE AT MY new job, I remember a time I was working on the computer at my cubicle and I looked up and saw our HR director lead a young woman about my age into his office. She stood out to me, with her navy suit and big smile. She seemed to glow. I knew she was something special, and I also knew she'd get the job she was seeking.

I was right. She was hired. Her name was Jennifer. If I had not taken this job, and if Jennifer had not been hired, this book would have a much different turn.

We became fast friends and often had lunch together. She was kind and wise. I learned she had a sick child, whom I grew to love very much. She also had tremendous faith. If it were not for the fact that I admired her and grew to trust her so much, I may have become weary of her high level of faith.

Turns out, I learned a lot from her about faith. She was careful not to come on too strong, but she gradually helped me to understand. I know how lucky I am to have met her.

Jennifer had a child who was gravely ill, and it didn't look promising for him. During this time she and some other faithful friends, family, and church members gathered around her son to "anoint him with oil" and pray for him. I was not invited, since she knew my faith was not yet strong enough. They all had to believe with their whole heart that God would cure her son in Jesus' name. Pretty deep stuff, I know. I tried to have an open mind about it all, but honestly, I really didn't know what to think of it. I sure hoped it would work.

As it turned out, doctors said it was a miracle when he showed an amazing turn around. Tests that only a few days before showed great problems were clear. She "witnessed" to me, as they say, and I took it all in. I admit, however, that I couldn't imagine how someone could have such strong faith.

Like many, I felt that *I* was always "in control" of my life. If I had a goal, I'd work hard to achieve it. I was usually successful in attaining my goals. It took me quite a while to learn who was really in control.

Jennifer and I were brought together on purpose. This is the reason I was hired to work for this company.

Jennifer and I spent a lot of time together. She was there when I was going through relationship struggles. She told me how I needed to put my life in God's hands. It sounds simple, but it was the greatest struggle in my life up to this point. She helped me every day by encouraging me to pray and ask for guidance. It took a while (OK, a *long* while), but this was the start of my faith journey.

The timing of Jennifer's entrance into my life came at a time when I needed her most. My maternal grandmother (the one who also was my godmother) passed away shortly before I met Jennifer. Jennifer filled my grandma's shoes in a way only she could.

Jennifer (left) and Diane (right)

CHAPTER 3

MY LIFE PARTNER

DURING MY RELATIONSHIP struggles, Jen continued to tell me to let go and let God take over. After a lot of internal struggles, I finally prayed my heart out to God and asked him to let something happen in the next week to show me the path I was to take. It wasn't your typical praying, but heart-wrenching, honest, and open. I shared with God everything that was in my heart. I figured, "OK, why not? It's worth a try, right?" I remember telling God as I prayed, "OK, you win. My life is in your hands." It was as if I surrendered to him. This may seem odd, but it was as if I was fighting him for a long time. I knew he was not 100% happy with the decisions I'd made up to that point. Instead I had chosen to look the other way and not face what God sought for me. At this time, I envisioned myself allowing God to take over, and I pictured myself being lifted up in his hands. Remember the commercial tag line, "You're in good hands with Allstate?" Yeah, it was like that.

About four days later, a series of circumstances took me out of the relationship with the person I had been with since my teenage years. I "happened" to have two vacation days left for the year and decided to get away from it all by going with my parents on a trip to see my (paternal) grandmother. My cousin, Susie, had just gone through a similar break-up, and since she lived in the same city, we took the road trip together. During the four-hour trip, Susie and I talked and cried and shared all our pain and the struggles we had encountered when our long-term relationships ended.

That weekend there was a big celebration going on where our grandmother lived and where Susie grew up. It changed my life.

When we first arrived at my grandmother's, I was tired and sad and not eating. I slept a lot and was not in the mood to clean myself up and attempt to look pretty. After Susie's pleading, she got me to go with her to attend the celebrations.

I was not in the mood to meet anyone, but that afternoon, while talking to my parents and Susie, I noticed this man who seemed to glow. (There's that word again.) OK, I know the word "glow" may sound a bit strange, but it's the best word to describe it. There were a lot of people around, but he stood out for some reason. It was as if God was saying, "Check him out!"

He disappeared into the crowd, and I didn't give him much more thought. That evening, during an outdoor concert Susie and I attended, I saw him again. I guided Susie to the spot I wanted to stand—next to him. I was glued there for some reason. Little did I know that he had spotted me earlier in the day and also "chose" to stand next to me. Even with his friend and Susie trying to get us to move, we continued to stand next to each other, and we eventually started up a conversation.

We ended up talking half the night. I was very aware of and cautious about members of the opposite sex, but for some reason I felt I could trust him. Later we gave Susie a ride home and continued to spend time together talking. He seemed intelligent and kind—not to mention, cute—and we seemed to have a lot in common. We discussed our careers and where we were from. Both of us had a passion for business and life. Most of all, he shared my faith.

He gave me his number, and based upon my current situation, he told me he'd let me make the decision if I wanted to pursue our relationship further. You guessed it—I followed up.

All of this within a week. I felt in my heart and soul that he was the one. I used to dream of a love like his, one that would make me feel secure and right. His name was Tim.

Our courtship was everything I ever dreamed. We did all of the things I had always wanted to do, and it was with someone who made *me* feel special. The time we spent together—from a picnic at "Picnic Point" to our strolls by the lake in downtown Madison—was filled with contentment. We talked about life and love and our careers and our families. We started planning our future together. We lived four hours from each other. Once, when we met in a city half way between our homes, we took a walk by a river. We talked about how we'd come back to that very same river some day after living a full and happy life together.

When things started to get more serious, Tim tested the waters with regards to our future. It never failed, if we were at the mall and "window shopped" at a jeweler, my hands would start to sweat. He'd gain ideas as to what I liked by pointing out different rings and watching my reaction.

The weekend he asked me to marry him started out pretty typical. We spent Saturday together, and then we went to a special restaurant for dinner. I started to get suspicious. Tim usually cooked dinner during my visits, but this time we'd gone to one of the nicest places in town. After dinner, we went back to his apartment and planned to watch a movie. Tim suggested I relax and change into comfy clothes. I put on an oversized sweatshirt and leggings. As I was waiting for him to join me in the family room, I heard him struggling in the other room, shuffling stuff and making noise. Soon he was on his knee asking me to spend the rest of our lives together. I started to cry. How could I say "no"?

Even though my parents were concerned about my "rebound" relationship, time proved everyone wrong. It is hard to convince people that God led me to him. Every time I prayed and asked God for direction with regards to Tim, I always felt a strong sense of approval and peace. How did I know? It's hard to explain. I just did. It's as if I was crystal clear with my decision. Have you ever tried to make an important decision on something but didn't quite know which direction to take? Personally, I believe if someone is waffling about a decision, it means the timing is not right. When the timing is right, the decision you make will be 100% clear, and there is only confidence and peace in it.

So I went with it. Just over a year later, we were married.

I did share with Tim some health challenges I had faced prior to our marriage. I had many issues with my reproductive system and told him there was a chance I would not be able to have children. He said he loved me and wanted to marry me regardless. We also decided that we would not prevent pregnancy once we were married so God could be in control.

The tough choice for us initially was deciding where to live. My company (now different from the one Jennifer and I had worked at) in Madison, Wisconsin, tried to recruit Tim when they heard of our engagement. However, Tim's company made him an offer he needed to pursue. We agreed that I would move. Since I had a lot of family in the area we were moving to, we would marry there as well. This was Kingsford, Michigan.

As we planned our wedding, Jennifer announced she was pregnant. I was so happy for her! Since she was my matron of honor, we were glad the timing would work out. We were planning a September wedding, and she was due in November.

I traveled back and forth from Madison to Kingsford as Tim and I planned our wedding, although he handled many of the details.

Our big day came quickly. A couple of days before our wedding, I drove back to Madison to drive Jennifer back up for the wedding. I didn't want her traveling alone in her condition.

We were married on a cold and rainy day in September. Despite the weather, the ceremony was beautiful. Many of my family members and friends from the Madison area made the trip to Michigan to join in our celebration.

After our wedding, I moved from Madison to the Kingsford/Iron Mountain area, and we found a little, two-bedroom home on a lake to rent. In our decision to move, Tim, knowing that Jennifer was a big part of my life, agreed to set aside a budget for long distance calls and frequent trips back home. He also supported my decision to be with her when her baby was born—shortly after our wedding. He knew how important it was for me to be there.

I will never forget the day Jennifer's beautiful second son was born. On November 1, 1990, Brandon was brought into the world. I was by her side during her labor and was the second person to hold little Brandon, as her husband held her hand during her after-birth. I sat on the rocking chair admiring his big, brown eyes and adorable face. He was perfect. He was healthy. What a blessing!

Leaving Jennifer after Brandon's birth was hard. We talked often, and I loved hearing how the boys were growing. I missed her, but we were always in each other's hearts.

CHAPTER 4

THROUGH SICKNESS AND IN HEALTH

I BELIEVE I WAS about 6 years old when I heard my mother talking to a friend about a woman who was unable to have children. I think they were saying something about a miscarriage and how the woman was not sure if she'd ever have children.

Running up to my room, I closed my door and cried. I couldn't imagine how sad it would be not to be able to have children. I remember praying and thinking how incredible it is to bring a baby into the world and how it was an experience I so desperately wanted to have someday.

Little did I know then how much this realization would affect me in the future. In the back of my mind, I worried, "What if that ever happens to me?"

The first few months of our marriage were great. We ended up moving again, this time to Marquette, MI. I got a job as an Account Executive (a.k.a. salesperson) at a local TV station, and Tim settled into a new position at a different company, with the same owners.

Things were going along nicely, but we soon learned what it meant to love each other through sickness and in health. I was having abdominal discomfort off and on. One night I was in such tremendous pain that Tim had to rush me to the ER. The doctors discovered a mass on my ovary, and I needed surgery to have it removed. It was scary. I had no idea what to expect, although since I'd had health issues in the past, nothing surprised me.

The experience of being a patient in this type of situation was difficult. I was dealing with so many emotions, and the hospital I went to was a training facility. As they were diagnosing my pain, my female doctor came in with a young intern. She asked me if he could "feel" the tumor on my ovary. I was very uncomfortable with the request, although I knew he was trying to learn. If he had the opportunity to learn from me, maybe it could help other women down the road. When he clumsily proceeded with the pelvic exam, it not only hurt, but also I felt violated. I have always been a very modest person, and it took everything in me not to kick him in the face and tell him to get the @%~# away from me. I held my breath until he was done, and I could feel my flushed face. It's one thing to go through surgery, but it's something entirely different when it also involves the private parts of your body.

The surgery was challenging. It sounded like I was unique in what she discovered. When I woke up from surgery, Tim was there, comforting me. I was still groggy, but he was trying to share the events of the surgery. The tumor was such a mess that they needed to not only remove it, but also my ovary and fallopian tube. It was difficult to take. I was scared about my future fertility. The doctor made it sound like my tumor was a fluke. She couldn't say if she suspected further challenges.

A year later, we moved back to Madison. Tim was seeking a position that was more challenging, and he was fortunate to find a position as a Computer Consultant. I found another sales position with a local TV station. Just as we were moving back to Madison, Jennifer was planning to move with her husband and boys to Austin, Texas, to be closer to her husband's family. It was tough saying good-bye again, but Jennifer knew I would be in good hands with Tim. I knew it would be good for her to have her husband's family close by. We knew we were forever bonded by heart.

Shortly after we moved to Madison and started new jobs, I once again ended up in the hospital. I now had a mass on my other ovary. This time, as I was wheeled into surgery, I was terrified I'd come out sterile. Again,

Tim was by my side and was only concerned about me. He never once expressed a concern about my not being able to have children. He kissed me and said he loved me—his eyes told me the rest. I continued into the operating room, and I closed my eyes and prayed hard that I could still have children when I woke up.

Tim was my rock.

When I awoke, I was fearful of hearing the same news that I'd heard the year before. Still coming out of anesthesia, I was groggy. It was a challenge to understand my discussion with the doctor. I do remember asking more than once if they were able to save my ovary. I was overjoyed and thanked God when I learned they were able to keep the rest of my reproductive organs intact. But we were told we'd need to follow an aggressive plan to take care of my health issues and to try to have children as soon as possible. I was also diagnosed with severe endometriosis (this is when the endometrial tissue that belongs in the uterus has adhered to other areas of the abdominal cavity). Apparently, this is what caused my issues with the original tumor. Back then, many doctors were not familiar with endometriosis. I was upset at the diagnosis, but relieved that they finally had a name for what I experienced.

Our plan started with my getting injections that would put my body into false menopause. Since I had severe endometriosis, I was told that the injections might help the disease go into remission long enough for us to try to have children. After a few months of it, I still needed surgery to remove the rest of the mass, and they removed half of my remaining ovary along with it. We were told it was still possible to have children if we could carefully manage the plans. We worked closely with a wonderful doctor named Jim Torhorst. He did everything he could to help us.

I forget just how many surgeries I've had. All I know is that I'm an "old hat" with them. My scars have been repeatedly re-opened. I have no feeling left where the scars are on my lower abdomen, as the entire "bikini line" area is numb. I have continuing issues with the scar tissue that has built up. It can be painful if I move too fast, but I can live with it.

A Prayer for the Future

Dear God of my future and my hope, I know you are
calling me forward and I'm learning slowly to trust
your great compassion and forgiveness.

I do not know where I'm going, but
I do know I want to do what is pleasing in your sight,
go where you want me to go.

I know that if I listen to my heart;
you will lead me by the right road;
though I may be surprised when I find myself on it.

I know I need not fear because you will never leave
me alone. I praise you for blessing me so richly. Keep
me faithful, God, now and forevermore. Amen.

—*Author Unknown*

CHAPTER 5

OUR JOURNEY — SNIPPETS FROM MY JOURNAL

IN THIS CHAPTER, I share various entries from the journal I kept as we went through our journey with infertility. Our journey lasted five years, but I only include entries that best string the story together. When I was going through infertility, I felt I was never going to be truly happy unless I was a mother. More than anything, I also felt as if I were the only one experiencing this pain. While I knew I should count my blessings and be satisfied with my life, my greatest desire was to be a mom. I refused to let go of my dreams.

I was never able to find books that really gave me what I wanted in terms of emotional validation. Some books covered the "how to" aspect of conception, but they did little to feed my emotional emptiness. I've written in journals since high school, and it has always been therapeutic for me. It was the way I could express my deepest feelings. I always felt better getting them off my chest.

We would have been happy to adopt, although the length of the process, the expense, and the possibility that the birth mother might change her mind made that option difficult. But first we wanted to explore how we could conceive and experience parenthood ourselves.

The entries I've chosen to share in this chapter are attempts to not only share my journey but also to disclose some of the emotions I experienced along the way. Someone reading this might truly understand what a woman going through infertility suffers, or if going through it herself, find validation. I apologize in advance for the entries that are hard to follow. There was a lot going on. You will also notice that at times I go from writing to my diary to talking to God.

October 28, 1991

Months have passed—not much has changed. Tim and I are happier than ever. Our saga continues as far as my body is concerned. This month I thought I might finally be pregnant. My cycles have been regular since my operation, and what else could I think? Well, I took one of those damn tests again, and once again it was negative. And really— that's OK—but once again, why didn't my cycle start? I just can't handle it sometimes. I felt like it was a cruel joke, and God, I know you love me and I have faith in you and I know whatever happens I can handle, but it's just hard. Poor Tim, he feels so bad when I'm down. I'm really OK about everything—I know things will be OK.

What is hard are the ongoing problems with my body. There is always something. Anyway, we'll be fine.

July 5, 1992

Well, I got my shot (this is the menopausal drug I spoke of in the previous chapter). It was a good 3 weeks ago now, but I'm getting a chance to write now. It was scary, getting the shot. All I could think about was that they were forcing a foreign drug into my body to cause my body to do unnatural things. I was so afraid. It's a new drug that hasn't been around long enough to know of any long-term effects. I just had to have blind faith in the doctors. I continue to try to hear God, to listen if he's trying to tell me to give all of this up and adopt, to help other women who are going through the same thing, or if he's trying to tell me to have faith and be patient and to use what the doctors have to bless me with a child.

I know from experience that sometimes you can be so blind to what God wants that you'll do anything to ignore the inevitable. Like deep down I might know I'm fighting a losing battle. But I don't think God would continue to give me false hopes. As Jennifer said, God left me my ovary

31

for a reason. He wouldn't keep stringing me along. He does know this last time, especially, I would have been strong enough to accept what I could not change. But my ovary was OK.

The endometriosis was quite a shock; I never really thought about it. Wow, I really have it. But ya know, there is a drug now that can help me that wasn't there 3 years ago. There is hope. God has told me all of my life that I would be a great mother, and I know he knows I realize and appreciate the miracle of birth. Conception to birth is the greatest miracle and blessing in the world. It's so sad that not everyone realizes that. Here I am, 24 years old, and I'm having hot flashes like a 55-year-old woman in menopause.

Melanie (sister-in-law) had a baby girl. Elina Nicole. She's so precious. I love her already. I've never really been there while an infant goes through the stages of growing up, and I find it fascinating. Everything she does intrigues me. From the way she hiccups, to her little scrunched up face when she cries, to her little smiles. Tim tells me just to be patient. God, please help me to be. All of my life I've rushed everything. Please help me to enjoy each day as it comes.

November 22, 1992

Life goes on. Well, lately I'm getting back to wanting to cry every time I get near a child. I guess as I get closer, the more afraid I become. As much as I hate to admit it, I do get scared thinking, "What if I can't get pregnant? Can I really handle it?" I really would be upset. I really would be mad. I would feel like an "it"—not a woman, an " it." And yes, I know Tim loves me, but it really would not be fair to him.

He married me, yes, but that was with the understanding that I was a woman, he a man, and we'd have a family.

I've been so moody and sensitive. One minute I think life is so great; the next minute I wonder what the point is to life. Of course, life is the people you love. Then we get back to children. I sound like a broken record.

November 29, 1992

Well, what more could go wrong? I broke my ankle. Yes, I really did. I still can't believe it. Tim and I went up north for Thanksgiving early Thursday morning. Friday, we drove to Marquette and had lunch with (an old client) Karen (that was great), then we went to Kevin and Melissa's (our good friends) and went to Casa for dinner and then the hockey game. On the way out I slipped on the ice and my ankle snapped.

(Note: Doctors diagnosed me with osteoporosis as a result of the medication, Lupron, that put me into my temporary menopause. Osteoporosis is one of the side effects and what caused my ankle to easily snap.)

December 13, 1992

Well, I have a lot of time on my hands while I'm recuperating from my surgery to "clean out" the endometriosis and while my ankle is broken. I thought I'd attempt to express some of the things going on in my head. My head is full of wonder and hope. I don't know where to begin. I want to be so close to God right now. I have no doubt that is by far the best feeling in the world. To have faith in God that he will lead Tim and me in the right direction. It has worked for us so far. It is an incredible feeling to have such strong faith, knowing that we are not alone in our life as Christians. It is such a comforting feeling. God, please help me to have complete faith in you, so we may follow your lead and head in the right direction.

I know I've been scared. I try to have 100% faith in you, God, and yet I know there are times when I think, "What if Tim and I don't get what we want?" I've been telling myself that even if we were to adopt, it would be OK. The child is still your child, and a gift to us, but I do want to experience the miracle of conception and birth. I get excited now that my operation is over, knowing the doctor said we should be OK. I saw the video-tape of my insides, and it seems like such a miracle that we could have a child. I have to stop worrying. I have to remember that many wonderful people we know were praying for us, and we got what we wanted in this step.

Now I can't stop thinking about each step we will take. First, we may be on fertility drugs; we can watch the development of my ovaries, and then watch when they give me a shot of HCG. I think about feeling symptoms of being pregnant. Could it really happen? I can't wait until the day I go to the doctor's and hear the nurse say, "Congratulations,

Diane, you are pregnant." I have it planned out how I would buy Tim a little present that would hint what I've found out.

I am so blessed to have a terrific husband and family and friends. Do I deserve a baby too? I think so. Because I know I would do well caring for a little person. I understand how much of a gift a child would be.

God, please help us.

You've done so much for us already. I hope I'm not being selfish by asking for a child. Please help me to become the best person I can be. Help me to continue to reach out and touch someone and to help other people. Please lead me in the right direction. My life is in your hands. It feels good to know I believe that. God, only you know the future for Tim and me. Please teach me patience.

Hard to remember

April 11, 1993

Well, I'm going to try to be deep and inspirational at the same time. I got my period again. But I think I may have learned something finally. When you think about it, life is so unpredictable. We can control a lot—what we say and do—but when you really stop and realize it, that's about all we control. You can't control if someone lives or dies; you can't control bringing life into the world; you can't control the weather, disease, illness, and what happens to the person you love.

Someone can enter the world and make an impact on many lives, but then they can be taken away just like that.

God controls everything. Whether or not we agree, we need to just have faith. You can't worry or fret over every little thing, because it won't matter.

Sometimes I feel like holding Tim hostage, holding him so tight that nothing can ever happen to him. I'm sure when we have children I'll feel the same way. But I can't. I have to just accept what happens in my life.

It is hard that I can't have a child. Part of me wants to cry and cry and wait until I am pregnant before I focus my life on anything else. Another part of me, (every) part of me wants to stop obsessing. Tim is supportive, but, God, it really is painful. More painful, 10 times more painful than physical pain.

No one has any idea of what all of this is like unless they go through it themselves. Of course, a lot of things in life are like that. Each family has their own special problems. Things could be much worse, and I must count my blessings.

May 9, 1993

Today is Mother's Day. We went to church in the morning. I was OK at first, and then all of a sudden, I became teary-eyed and upset. There was a pregnant woman sitting in front of us and a newborn baby girl next to us. I just couldn't control my emotions.

I looked in my purse for a tissue, and right at the end of church I was dabbing my eyes. On the way out, a man was handing out carnations to all the mothers. I tried not to make eye contact and attempted to walk right past. He followed me and said, "You didn't get a flower." I said, "Oh, no thank you." A couple of seconds later I was crying in the lobby of the church. I tried to cover my face and run downstairs to the ladies' room, but I couldn't. So I tried to get myself together. I walked around, trying to get away from people. Then a woman asked if I was looking for the first graders!

I felt like, "I'm not deserving of a child, and I don't deserve a flower." I was crying and crying. Tim was great. I wish I wouldn't have broken down like that; I really couldn't control it. I'm better now.

I didn't write before, but Dr. Torhorst wants to put me on 2 pills/day next month. I started in February with all of this.

June 10, 1993

Here I am at home on a Thursday, at one in the afternoon. I feel like calling in sick this afternoon because I'm depressed.

I am obsessed with having a child. It won't change until I have a child. This pain is like no other pain—it burns in your heart like a hole. I don't know if I could handle not being able to have children . . .

I'm better now. I didn't really explain before, but my endometriosis made a come back. It only took 6 months. That is why we are coming down to the wire.

July 7, 1993

I wonder if I've done myself any good. I bought a book on endometriosis. I really need God to be here with us right now to help answer some questions. I feel more informed, and then I wonder if my doctor should be doing more. If I am ovulating every month, if my tube is clear, why am I not getting pregnant? He says to give it a year. OK, fine, but then he says maybe we should try in-vitro. I'm wondering—isn't there another problem we are not considering?

I read stories by other women, and I want to tell mine. I found so many answers to my questions: Why am I always tired and have no energy? That is a complaint of the majority of women with endometriosis. I assumed I was just lazy. Unbelievable. I also believe it was inevitable from birth. I have had symptoms since I first menstruated. I wonder if all of the times my system would be "backed up" with my cycles, if that is what caused the flow back up through my tubes.

I read of another hormone that causes contractions. It is created in the endometrium and women with endometriosis have more endometrium and therefore have more of the contraction-inducing hormone and that can cause miscarriage. I have so many questions. Will I ever get pregnant? Will I just be another statistic? God determines this. What has he chosen for me?

I'm not sure what direction to go. Do I try to see another doctor who is an expert in the field? Do I risk not being covered by an insurance company? What if Tim changes jobs and I have to be turned down due to a pre-existing condition? I am so scared, God. It's not fair that people with illnesses have to go it alone. It is so hard for them, and it's almost as if people with illnesses that they cannot control are being punished.

I believe I must put my life into God's hands—completely. Have total faith. I will also try to help myself. God gave us doctors and people to help us, so I will take advantage of it.

My cycle is now on day 30. I got a headache and a mid backache yesterday, so I'm calculating I'll be starting tomorrow.

I can't help feeling like I'm depriving Tim of his chance to be a father. Yes, I know he loves me, but I can't help feeling that way. He deserves a child of his own flesh and blood.

Some days my heart is in the pit of my stomach, and I'm so sad that I can't (yet) get pregnant. I don't feel like a true woman. If I let myself, I could just hide away and be depressed all the time. But I can't do that! That is the only bad thing in my life. I have to remember that I'm so happy otherwise to have Tim. Then I keep thinking how I want to be able to give him a child to make it complete.

Well, I am going to fight! This disease is not going to ruin me. God, tell me what direction to go.

Hopefully I didn't lose you completely with the journal entries. While I've always been described as being someone who wears her heart on her sleeve as well as being an "open book," it is not easy sharing the depths of my emotions. My ultimate goal is always to help others. If sharing offers help, I'm OK with it. For people to hang on to hope, they also need to know just how far down someone can get and yet still achieve hope.

Now I'll continue my story.

After a few months on a fertility drug to help us get pregnant, we had no luck. We were both doing well with our careers. We were achieving our goals, except the one that was most important to me—having children. I wanted what I wanted and that was that. It was as if I would make it happen with or without God.

We finally decided to try in-vitro fertilization (IVF) to conceive. Dr. Torhorst, my regular OB/GYN, who specialized in basic infertility treatment, knew that we had gone as far as we could with him. He cared so much about helping us to be parents that he shared it was time for us to move to the next step, but it did not include him. He recommended a top doctor who not only specialized in infertility but also endometriosis. He was two and a half hours from where we lived. I would have another surgery, and then we started our journey to make a baby.

When we started the entire process of trying to get pregnant, I didn't think we would go this far. Part of me felt that if God wanted us to have a child, he would make it happen. Part of me also knew that God gave us doctors to help us. Either way, it was up to God, not us. Admittedly, I remember praying for what I wanted, but not really listening to God or, for that matter, trusting God.

I felt torn, as if I knew we didn't have God's blessing, but we still plowed forward. Remember what I said earlier about making decisions? On the surface, I convinced myself that since I was praying throughout the process, God would answer our prayers, yet it was hard to tell if what we were embarking on was our will or God's will.

We experienced many obstacles along the way: big snow storms, our vehicle breaking down on the highway, and many stresses. I worried, "What if it doesn't work? It *has* to work!" and "What if it works so well that I have 5 babies? What if they didn't survive?" I prayed and prayed, but again, I made the decision without God's blessing. Deep down I knew this. Tim supported me, and he wanted me to be happy. Here are more journal entries that share this experience.

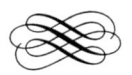

December 18, 1993

We are going for it (IVF)! We went to see a specialist in Lake Forest, Illinois. Everything happened quickly. We went down on a Monday (12/13) and returned for a laparoscopy on Thursday (12/16). I saw it all on video-tape afterwards. They just kept burning away the bad parts. Literally. It was hard to look at. What will be left of my pelvic area if they continue to do that? It's such a shame. My body is a gift from God. Because of this awful disease, it's taking away more and more. It's not deadly at this point, but down the road?

We are going to try in-vitro fertilization. It's exciting and scary, but I'm going to remain positive. There is no reason it shouldn't work. Next month, we will start. It's expensive—$10,000 for one try. Insurance won't cover any of it. I'll have to be off of work for a week or more, but ya know, it's all going to be worth it.

February 8, 1994

We started with the Lupron shots yesterday. I am so excited! I may be pregnant in one month. Wow, that is coming up! I'm so happy. Tim was so incredibly loving. He was trying to be so careful when he gave me the shot. I have a bruise on both hips/thighs from the shot sites.

February 28, 1994

Here we are! Ready to conceive our baby(ies). Everything is going well. I'm on day 11 of my cycle, and tonight I will (should) get my HCG shot. Wednesday will be the egg retrieval and Friday the transfer. I now may have 12 follicles. For one (1/2) an ovary, they say that's great! My estrodial ? *level is over 1,000, so that's good, and my lining is plump. I started stimulation Sunday of last week in Madison. Dr. Torhorst's nurse Diane came in on a Sunday for me. Then we continued in Madison Monday and Tuesday. On Wednesday, Tim and I drove in a big snowstorm to Chicago. That night, on the way home just by the Stoughton exit, our Bravada broke down. We had to wait almost 2 hours to make it home, to wait for the tow truck and then the cab. The fuel line was the problem, so it's OK now. Thursday, Mom and I drove down and planned to stay overnight at (my friend) Dawn's apartment. Then Friday, another snowstorm hit, so Mom and I ended up staying over Friday also. Originally Mom and I were to drive back Friday, to give me my afternoon shot at home, and Tim and I would drive back Saturday morning, but they did not allow it now. The weather was so bad we got stuck in snow by Dawn's apartment. We'd get pushed a foot, and we'd get stuck again and again. We had fun, talked a lot, and had some time to be alone. Dawn went to stay with her old roommate, so mom and I had her place together. It was a cute apartment. She had her bears all over the place, decorated very nicely.*

March 1, 1994

My head is spinning, and I'm going stir crazy cooped up in this apartment (stayed there during IVF in Lake Forest).

I'm so excited about the possibilities. I may be pregnant in less than one week. It's been a yo-yo goal—having children. We've been trying so long to get pregnant. Last night I got my HCG shot. Tim and I had to go to the emergency room to find the nursing supervisor to give me the shot. My retrieval is tomorrow!

March 4, 1994

I had my transfer today. It went well. I was so scared and embarrassed; (some detail omitted, I am a very private person on this subject).... I said, "I don't know if I can do this!" They were great and told me everything. It did hurt though. Then I had to lie on my stomach for 3 hours. That was tough. There were also 3 other women who had their transfers. Lying there was hard because they had a rock-hard pillow that hurt my face, and my lower back was so sore! When I got home I had to spend the rest of the day in bed. I couldn't even raise my head. It will all be worth it. But I'm scared to do anything! I'm responsible for my potential baby(ies). When I go to the bathroom I'm afraid they'll fall out, or when I cough or sneeze or laugh, even though they say not to worry. I just need to relax. Please, God, help me to. There is so much to worry about if I let myself. I do feel vulnerable now because I'm not only responsible for myself but also the baby(ies).

March 13, 1994

I have my pregnancy test in 2 days. I am so scared. Our future depends on this test. It just hit me—what if

I'm not pregnant? I've been on such a roller coaster. I try to prepare myself.

The day we were supposed to get the call to learn if I was pregnant (after much stress and a large investment), I came home from work about 2:45 p.m. The doctor was to call at 3 p.m. Tim was going to meet me at home.

The phone rang earlier than I expected. I thought it was Tim saying he was on his way. It was the doctor's office.

The result was "negative."

It was good Tim was not home yet. I remember crying and sobbing loudly. I felt beaten down. I kept screaming, *"Why?"* At the same time I also screamed, "I am still with you, God. Nothing will keep me from you. I can handle it. Please help me!" I was in great pain, yet I distinctly remember feeling like a fighter in a boxing ring. I was not going to give up on God or my dreams. My faith was certainly tested.

When Tim walked in moments later, he looked at my face and knew. He held me as I cried. There was little either one of us could say.

I was so distraught and depressed. I felt I needed something to care for, so I pleaded with Tim to let me buy a dog. My friend and coworker, Mary, and I happened to stop into a pet store, and I immediately fell in love with a little Bichon/Cocker puppy. He was adorable. He would get up on his back legs and "doggy paddle" his front legs in excitement. Tim gave in, and it helped to fill me up a little.

At Tim's suggestion, we named the puppy "Otis." The first few nights we had him, he would go into his kennel and lie down all by himself. This reminded Tim of the character Otis on *The Andy Griffith Show* who apparently returned to his jail cell by himself. I agreed that "Otis" had a cute ring to it. Otis, however, became very sick early on, and I will never forget a terrifying dream I had soon after.

Before you read this, I warn you, this is kind of spooky. In my nightmare, I was sleeping. Four evil spirits swooped into my room, paralyzed me, and tried to suffocate me to stop me from screaming for help. The spirits then swooped inside of me (through my birth canal) and took out my embryos. Then they went after my new little puppy. In my dream I tried to scream and couldn't. Then I woke up. It was terrifying! After great thought and discussions with other spiritual friends, we decided it was symbolic of my fear of my situation. When someone fears, he or she does not completely trust God, and Satan has an advantage over that person. I know, deep stuff. By the way, Otis did get better. Whew!

When we met with the doctor to review why the IVF failed, he was shaking his head. He said he didn't know why this happened. Statistically, we were perfect candidates. As we spoke in his office, I was eager to move forward. I quietly cried as he shared that first I'd need to have injections again for several months. I felt as if we were climbing Mount Everest all over again.

April 17, 1994

We had our follow up-appointment yesterday. It wasn't at all what I expected. They said they wouldn't recommend transferring the two frozen embryos, as once thawed the chance of survival is 50%. It seems as though we are starting all over again. He thought I might have to be on Lupron to suppress any endometriosis growth and then do IVF again. They are also surprised that IVF did not work. They said there may be a chance I have something where Tim's blood and mine are too similar. My body might not recognize the fetus, and therefore it would not implant. Since everything went so well every step of the way—they thought we should check into that. I broke down crying when he said we'd have to start all over with Lupron, etc. It's so hard!

Sometimes I wonder if we should just throw in the towel. But then I think that if it works it will all be worth it. I told my mom I feel like I'm staring in a book or watching a movie about a woman who goes through everything imaginable to have a child. I can't let go of the possibilities. However, I'm not ready to admit it will never happen. My head is spinning about everything. I have to be patient and take it one day at a time, all the while accepting and being happy the way things are. I expected IVF to be the last step down our infertility road, but once again we're at the beginning. We decided I should write a book to help others someday, except I'm still waiting for a happy ending. The not knowing is the hardest. I thought this would determine one way or another and then we could go on. But so many things about the first IVF attempt were so good we were so close! Then we get a little closer to solving the mystery.

CHAPTER 6

LEARNING
TO TRUST GOD

JENNIFER, MY DEAR friend, was supporting me through all of this, but she knew I still did not have complete faith in God. One blessed day, there was an opportunity for me to take a short trip with her and her parents, who are equally faithful. I remember our long talk as they discussed what faith is. They told me you can believe in God without having complete faith. They knew I was fearful that my dreams might not come true. They told me fear is not of God—it is from Satan. I'd never really talked about Satan before. I knew he existed, but I never talked about him, as it seemed too "out there." I felt horrible that I was allowing Satan to control my emotions. I felt as if I was being "scolded" for not having complete faith. This goes back to my nightmare after we got our puppy.

When Jennifer's parents told me this, I was confused. I wanted to trust completely! "*How* do you learn to trust completely?" I asked. I listened intently and thought long and hard about what they said.

That night as I prayed, I decided to open up to God completely. I asked him for forgiveness for my being afraid and asked him to show me how to have complete faith.

Shortly after this realization (of what it really is to have faith in God), we were getting closer to the time we needed to start the entire infertility process up again. During this time, I found a wonderful counselor who not only helped me emotionally, but also spiritually. I took a "cram course" to get to where I needed to be spiritually before we tried to move forward with our plans.

I learned that our worries can be given over to the Lord. It is easier said than done, and some readers may think it all seems too hard to grasp. I thought the same thing. People told me about other women they knew who could not have children and then ended up with four. It seemed unreal, and I could only wish. I remember being so desperate to talk to someone who knew what I was going through with my endometriosis. A good friend and coworker gave me the number of someone who also went through it and had since had three kids. The woman was gracious enough to talk to me, although it was difficult to talk with her screaming kids in the background. I wished that would be me someday.

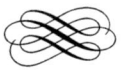

July 10, 1994

I passed a woman as I left the library the other day. She was dressed casually, with two young children in tow. I was on my lunch break from work and dressed in a business suit. She looked at me and gave me the up and down, while I looked at her with a half smile. It's like she was thinking, "Oh look at her—selfish and out for the almighty buck, probably childless or one of "those" women who leave her child(ren) with a day-care provider." Or, "That's where I would be if I didn't have children."

I looked at her with envy, wondering if she really appreciated her children, as I tucked my books about infertility under my arm.

People just don't understand. They say, "I don't have children, and it doesn't bother me if I see a baby." I tell them, "Nor do they want children." I'm tired of people telling me I'm foolish for the way I feel.

July 21, 1994

We watched a TV show last night on "Now with Tom and Katie" about in-vitro fertilization and how the strong use of fertility drugs causes cancer of the ovary, possibly increasing the chances by 37%. Of course, most likely I'll have my other ovary yanked out of my body someday with my uterus. The idea of a hysterectomy tears me up inside.

I can hardly handle it. It's so hard if I think about it too much. I think I may go crazy or get depressed. Life is very hard. I never wanted or expected to have health problems. Our society does not have time for problems like I have. They make me feel like a wimp, like there is no time to cry. You need to work to make money; you need to be "up" for everyone else; you can't cry; it's silly to feel that way; women were not put on this earth just to have children.

It's my worst nightmare coming true. I have to stay "up" and do it on my own with God's strength.

August 1, 1994

I wanted to take time and write about my recent discoveries. I talked to the pastor last Tuesday about all of the anxiety I've been feeling about my infertility. He was some help, I guess. He reinforced my feelings (and my love for Tim) about how much I am blessed by having him in my life. I really know that I am lucky to be married to him and to have such incredible friends and family. He also said I have to take my worries and hand them over to God and let God take care of everything. He also said he believes that God doesn't make bad things happen to us, instead, he is there when things are hard and helps by offering choices to us; and that God knows us so well that he knows what our choice will be. I said that God obviously knows I'll do anything to have a child.

Jennifer is in town right now. It's nice to see her again. She helped me, as always. She said how fear is of Satan and how I have to face Satan and let him know that I am God's child. Satan can't touch me. My unborn children are God's children, and Satan can't touch them. Confronting Satan is better than pretending he does not exist. She gave me Psalm 91 to read, which talks of how God will protect us. Psalm 91:2–7 says:

I will say of the Lord, "He is my refuge and my fortress, my God, in whom I trust." Surely he will save you from the fowler's snare and from the deadly pestilence. He will cover you with his feathers, and under his wings you will find refuge; his faithfulness will be your shield and rampart. You will not fear the terror of the night, nor the arrow that flies by day, nor the pestilence that stalks in the darkness, nor the plague that destroys at midday. A thousand may fall at your side, ten thousand at your right hand, but it will not come near you.

God will bless Tim and me with a child. Because he knows my heart, that I want to experience the true miracle of birth, he will present me with choices as to how we will achieve our goal. We need to pray about our choices and move on and continue to be guided by our faith.

August 13, 1994

I have many things to be happy about, but I feel I'm losing control sometimes as far as my body is concerned. I can't believe what is going on in my body! I had another doctor's appointment on Wednesday, and Dr. Torhorst basically said my body is a mess. I have no control over this disease—of course no one really ever does when it comes to diseases. I wonder how many people think I may have "caught" this disease. I never really thought about it before, but I don't have to worry about something else. My eyes—I'm so blind and vulnerable without my contacts—my ankle and how I may never "dance" again, and of course my reproductive system and my infertility.

I'm in pain more often lately, and it's unusual since I've been on Lupron for the last 3 months—all of this also affects the intimacy in our marriage. I am so tired of it all!

You go along in life doing what you're supposed to—being a good person and taking a day at a time. Then all of a sudden one day you realize you're not as healthy as you used to be. You wonder what happened and when. The longer you live, the more pain you experience. That's what they mean when they say, "That's life!"

When parents look at their precious baby just minutes old, they can't help but wonder what trials and challenges he or she will face as he or she ventures down the road of life. Who knew when I was a child all I'd have to go through to have one of my own?

October 17, 1994

Looks like I'm finally getting a chance to write! It's amazing how I have to take a day off from work to get the opportunity!

Where do I start? I found a lump in my left breast. I saw Dr. Torhorst a week and a half ago. He felt it and said he thinks it's a swollen gland and not to worry about it, but to wait about a month and see if it goes away—unless it gets bigger. Then I should go in and have a biopsy done. I check it off and on. One day it seems smaller and the next bigger. I don't know!

Then I worry, "What if I had breast cancer, and what if I die?"

It has all shown me how to appreciate my life more. I have a tendency to think about everyone else all the time, thinking my life and my body can't take me down. But I have to admit that with all the things I've done to my body to try to have a baby, it does worry me. All the things that are not tested for long-term effects. When I had the first Lupron shot I cried—like I was trying to tell myself something. I remember how scared I was to put a new, unnatural drug into my body. I worried about the long-term effects. Then being on it again! Most women are on it only one time, and I've been on it two times. I just have to go on blind faith. I felt like I had no choice. It was either that or have a hysterectomy. I feel like my body has gone to war and back again. I'm only 27. I'm thankful I have God in my life and Tim and my parents and my friends. I've been very blessed that way.

I must remain positive. Eventually something good will come out of all of this! I may just have a swollen gland.

(Note: It was just a swollen gland. The doctor was right.)

November 1994

Wow! Today as I write this I'm a page deeper in my journal. I wonder about all that will have happened in my life by the time these pages are filled.

I had the most extraordinary dream last night. I was about 3-4 months pregnant, and I was into the doctor to have an ultrasound done. Tim and I were elated, and we cried and cried. I had apparently conceived in January, and the baby had Tim's nose in the ultrasound. My concern was for the baby, and I was worried that something might go wrong. Then I realized that God will protect my life and our child's life. The only way one can get through life is to hand it over to God completely.

Oh, God, please forgive me for not trusting you completely. I do in every area, yet I question you when it comes to the baby thing. I'm so sorry; you know what my heart's desire is. I believe you will lead me there. The thought of having a child growing inside of me—it would be like being in heaven. I can't begin to explain the absolute happiness I felt in my dream. I think you may have been trying to tell me something.

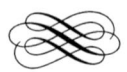

My spiritual counselor taught me a symbolic ritual on how to "give my concerns to the Lord." She told me to write down all of my worries on a piece of paper, burn it, and do something special with the ashes. I put the ashes into a favorite plant. She explained that as the paper burned and the smoke rose, it symbolized my worries being carried to God. It's almost like a child putting his or her worries on a parent. As if the child opens up to the parent about something and the parent solves it and "makes it all better." I said a prayer and asked God to handle all my worries. I also told him I trusted him to take care of things for me. As a child trusts a parent.

One time I forced myself to "be still" after praying to God so I could actually attempt to listen to him. I heard this is one of the biggest obstacles people have when trying to connect with God. They are never "still" and never take time to really listen. I thought I'd give it a try.

First, I took the day off from work so I could focus on connecting with God. I like to talk to God as if he is my best friend, just as I've done most of my life. Anything that was bothering me, I'd just start praying and talking to him about everything going on in my head. I never really heard him talk back to me, but I do think I felt his presence. This day, I went into my room and made sure all was quiet. I poured my heart out to God and told him everything. You know, you can't trick God. He knows your heart. I tried to be honest with him. I asked him to forgive me for not trusting in him 100%. I told him how he couldn't blame me for being fearful. I was born that way, like everyone else, yet I was trying, and I wanted him to help me. I told him I would really like for him to give me a sign or talk to me and that I was "all ears."

Yes, I had to try hard! My mind kept wandering from projects I needed to get done at work, to the next doctor's appointment, to my sore shoulders, and more! But then an amazing thing happened. A "voice" popped into my head that said, "I will put you at peace." I was amazed and excited and scared all at the same time. There was no doubt in my mind it was God. I know this sounds hard to believe. I would have been skeptical myself, except it really happened to me.

It didn't make a lot of sense, which confirmed to me that I hadn't put the thought into my head. I knew God had spoken to me. At first I didn't know what he meant—I thought, "Does he mean I will be going to heaven?" "Does it mean he will give me peace somehow?" I eventually realized it meant I would have a child and be at peace. How did I know this? I just did.

Shortly after this, Tim and I were in church, listening to the church school's Christmas program. Typically, this would have brought me pain, as I would have watched the precious children and worried that I would never experience my own. This day I was filled with peace and hope, and I took with me the knowledge that someday our own child(ren) would be up there singing. While the children were singing "Little Drummer Boy," God spoke to me again, out of the blue, and said, "It's coming." I was overjoyed, and my heart was swollen and happy.

December 5, 1994

I prayed last night and asked God to give me a sign of what was to come as far as the baby thing goes. I asked him to help me stay calm through our decisions and to lead us in the right direction.

This morning at church, my heart was filled with overwhelming love, like God was telling me we have happiness coming to us very soon. He didn't say how, but he promised me it's coming. One way or another.

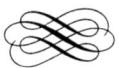

When we went through our second IVF attempt, this time I knew God was with me. I could feel Jesus' presence as the doctors did what they needed to do. This time around, we went with a local doctor, who also agreed that the husband can be involved in giving the shots, rather than having to make trips twice daily to the clinic. It was a time of bonding, and the timing was always crucial. The first time Tim had to give me an injection, it hurt him more than me. Luckily, with all of my past surgeries for endometriosis, I was tough as nails when it came to the shots. Did I ever bruise from some of them! Tim always felt bad, seeing the bruises in spots from prior shots, and yet he had to keep giving them. He was a pro, though.

While I knew I would get pregnant this time, I was also willing to accept anything that would be coming my way. If for some reason I was wrong and did not conceive, we were ready to adopt. We knew every child is a gift from God, regardless if it came from my body or not. I realized that God is in control and knows what is best. Either way, I was ready and was at peace and stress free. This is so important for anyone trying to get pregnant. Stress can be a major deterrent in getting pregnant, but it was as if my body (and soul) were "ready."

January 22, 1995

We are starting another IVF cycle in Madison. It will be nice to be in Madison this time—less stressful.

I've been trying very hard to relax this time. I'm even going to a friend's therapist. She's very good. We've determined that I definitely internalize my stress right to my uterus. She says it's as if my body is compensating for my emotions. When I talk about my feelings or beliefs etc., I tense all up inside.

She's going to try to teach me relaxation techniques. She also suggested I have a hard time accepting "gifts" since I'm such a giver. She said when you're giving, you are in control and you're not vulnerable. Yet when you are receiving, you are vulnerable. She said the ultimate test or reciprocal gift would be a child from God. She had me visualize what I would feel to become pregnant, and I discovered that, in addition to being thrilled, I'd be scared of the responsibility of caring for the baby inside. I'd be feeling vulnerable. Now if something happens to me—I get sick, get shot, hit by a car—it's just me. I'm tough, and I survive. But if there is a baby inside, that's when I have to have complete trust in God.

Please, Jesus, fill me up with your love and faithfulness. Give me strength to overcome my fears.

January 29, 1995

We started the IVF process yesterday. Although yesterday I was a bit stressed about a few things, I'm doing better now. I think it is less stressful that we are able to give the shots ourselves. It's 2 times a day, AM and PM, and Tim's been giving me the shots. Once you get the hang of it, it's actually not so bad.

I'm not thinking about it now. I'm letting God take care of that. I'm going to do everything I can this time to make sure I'm in tip-top shape in mind, body, and soul. Then if it still does not work, at least I gave it my best shot. But God told me it's coming, and I believe him.

I keep thinking there is so much to learn in life if you just seek. I feel I can look at the big picture of life.

Tim's been supportive of my therapist. She is a great lady. I feel selfish sometimes, like I'm paying her to listen to me, but there are many things she's helping me with.

I saw Annie today (she's my friend who's trying to become a mom too). God I pray you help her attain her goal and you lead her in the right direction.

February 7, 1995

Hello! I'm writing about our 2nd IVF experience so far. My follicles were stimulated quite rapidly this time—8 days of Pergonal and Metrodin. We got the HCG shot last Saturday night and yesterday had the egg retrieval. They didn't knock me out for it, so I was scared of what to expect. I was shaking violently on the operating table before they started. I didn't think I'd be able to make it through. But then I relaxed. Yes, it hurt, but almost in a good way, because I knew it resulted in getting an egg.

February 10, 1995

I'm back. Everything went well! They got 12 eggs versus 8 last time and fertilized 10. They transferred 6.

Yikes! But I'm at peace about it. They originally thought they fertilized 9, and one fertilized after the initial ones did, so they decided to just stick them all in.

I'm excited this time. I know it's going to work. The question is, how many? I'm not even scared; the Lord took away my fear. I've had no cramping or spotting either!

February 15, 1995

Five more days till the pregnancy test. It's weird. I just wait and hope. I've been home for a week and ½ now. I plan to go back to work tomorrow, maybe for a ½ day. My baby(ies) should be implanted by now. I've had some problems with hyper stimulation, but not really severe. I went to the doctor yesterday AM because I was having some trouble breathing, but they said it's OK. Apparently the follicles push up against your diaphragm, and I feel like I do after a laparoscopy.

I'm doing OK in terms of the waiting, but I'm finally realizing that whatever is meant to be, will be. God knows what is best. Period. I have many people praying for me, and I've gotten so much strength from God. I feel his presence and/or the presence of his angels with me whenever I've needed it.

He's been walking with me this time, and he's been there every step of the way. I feel so blessed, and I know God loves me. No matter what. Still no cramping!

CHAPTER 7

THE CALL

WHEN WE WERE to get "the call" this time, I asked Tim to come home early. The plan was for me to stay in our bedroom. I would unplug the phone, and he could answer it downstairs, so I wouldn't hear the phone ring.

I didn't know they'd called when Tim came into the room with a strange look on his face. "It's positive," he said. He didn't jump for joy or swing me around the room like I had imagined he would. Instead, he was very cautious. The last thing he wanted was for me to experience any more "blows." The doctor told Tim the chance for miscarriage this early is great. Tim didn't want us to tell too many people yet. I knew his faith is one of "everything happens for a reason." If things *did* happen, we'd survive because God is there for us. I recently learned, however, what it means for God to tell you something and then for a person to trust his word.

I was completely elated with the news and felt like I was on "cloud nine."

February 20, 1995

I'm just shaking. It's 3 p.m. and the doctor is supposed to call after 3 p.m. to tell me if I'm pregnant or not.

My entire future depends on this call. The next time I write it will be good news or sad news. Please God, I feel you promised it's coming. I pray it's true and I heard you correctly.

Tim may be coming into the bedroom any minute with a smile or a sad face. I will know just by looking at him.

IT'S YES!!

Thank you, God! I praise you and will never forget what you've done!

March 6, 1995

We had our ultrasound today. It looks like we have one baby! We are so happy. Tim and I had such a great weekend. The next two weeks are most susceptible to miscarriage. I was a little worried at first, but not anymore. God will take care of us and our unborn baby.

I'm so excited! I still cannot believe it! Thank you, God, and please be there to protect your baby every step.

9 weeks pregnant

We saw the baby wiggle this time! It was incredible to say the least. We saw it's head, tummy, arms, and legs. I'm still in awe and shock!

Dr. Torhorst said the baby's perfect. It has a healthy heartbeat. I'm thrilled! He said I have a low lying placenta, but it usually moves up as the pregnancy progresses. Thank you, God!

April 23, 1995

Almost 13 weeks. I can't believe it's been so long since I've written! I'm so tired all the time. It's such a beautiful morning—the window is open to the bedroom, the sun is shining, and the house is clean!

The exciting news—I felt the baby kick on Easter Sunday, in the evening! It was wonderful. I'm so proud of our little one. We announced the pregnancy on Easter. Dean cried. Everyone was so happy for us. Darla (sister-in-law) also cried. Mom got us an Easter basket with a bunch of baby things inside. Brian and Sally(cousin and his wife) sent us a "bunny" bib. I'm so excited! It's still hard to imagine actually having our dream come true and having our baby in our home and in our lives. But we are on our way, and it's actually going to happen.

There were so many exciting times in my pregnancy, but one that stood out to me the most is the way my brother, Dean, reacted to the news. There had been a couple of times since Tim and I married when he'd asked if we were going to have children. I finally told him that I didn't know if I could. I opened up about how difficult it was for me because we wanted children so badly. This was on the phone, and I could tell he felt really bad for us. I asked him to say a prayer for us. I know he did.

The end of April, my parents, Tim, and I celebrated my brother's birthday. We signed his card, "Love Diane, Tim, and baby." He took a moment to read it, and he really studied it to make sure he understood what we were saying. He buried his face in his hands and cried with joy. I cried too. I knew how happy he was for us and how excited he was to be an uncle. I was three months pregnant at the time, and the baby was growing "beautifully." I cannot describe my complete joy and contentment.

We had many ultrasounds with my pregnancy, as I was diagnosed with "placenta previa." This is when the placenta that nourishes the baby covers the cervix, thus not giving the baby a way out. My doctor was concerned about me dilating, as I might start as early as twenty-six weeks. In my condition, there was a great risk of hemorrhaging. He explained it can be a balancing act between the baby and the mother. If the bleeding is too much, the mother might bleed to death (the placenta gradually tears away from the uterine wall as dilation occurs). If you take the baby too early, it could be harmful for the baby.

I was not allowed to be more than thirty minutes from the hospital at any time. I was told to "take it easy" at work and had to constantly ask coworkers to trek up a flight of stairs for me to deliver paperwork, had to cancel appointments out of town, etc. In the end, my doctor said I had the "perfect" placenta previa. They planned a scheduled C-section as soon as it was safe for the baby to be born—three weeks prior to my official due date.

July 25, 1995

Things are going wonderfully! We had another ultrasound on Friday. Dr. Torhorst said everything is perfect with the baby. The only problem is the placenta previa. I've been a little concerned about that.

Our lives are in God's hands. I trust he'll take care of us. By the ultrasound, it looks like we are having a beautiful little girl! All we ask is for our child to be healthy.

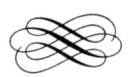

There were some wonderful baby showers put on by my dear friends, coworkers, and family. My friend Laura, who was also my roommate in college, put on my first baby shower, along with help from my friends Paula and Melissa. It was held at my house, because they lived more than thirty minutes from the hospital. It was very nice. My coworkers, Minde, Milissa, Mary, Susan, Sara, Pam, Darcy, and others planned another one (thanks for letting me try to mention everyone by name!). Everyone was so happy for us. They'd been with me through thick and thin as we tried to conceive. Milissa, in fact, always told me she knew I'd have a child someday. During a time I was particularly distraught, she'd even bought me a special "Precious Moments" figurine that said, "Dreams Really do Come True." It meant a lot.

My parents and my cousin's wife, Sally, had another shower at my parents' hobby farm. After so long, it seemed overwhelming to think everyone was there celebrating our baby's pending birth. Another shower was planned for after the birth through Tim's family.

The Friday before our baby was born, I was walking into a deli shop to pick up subs. I'd seen the doctor that day, he'd decided that the following Monday would be the day I would have the baby. I must have been walking on sunshine (with a smile from ear to ear), as a woman stopped me and told me I must have been *the* happiest pregnant woman she'd ever seen. I was quite big by that time, and most women are uncomfortable by that point. I shared with her that I'd just learned I was going to have my baby on Monday and that after so many years of trying, I was very excited. I didn't complain once (at least I don't think I did). I took each and every aspect of my pregnancy with great appreciation.

The C-section was a bit nerve-wracking, as I had started hemorrhaging. I made Tim promise to stay with the baby. With the reports we used to hear about "baby switches," etc., there was no way I wanted our baby out of my sight. I couldn't see anything because they had blocked my view, but I felt some tugging and pressure (due to the epidural). It was the strangest feeling not being able to move my lower body. I could see them maneuver my legs around, and it was as if they had some rubber legs right next to mine and were moving them. Such an odd feeling. Finally, I heard the most beautiful sound in the world. My precious miracle baby—*She* was crying. I was in such awe, and I was so happy I didn't quite know what to do with myself. I couldn't believe I had a baby! We really had a baby!

Tim followed her as she was getting checked out, and Dr. Torhorst was working feverously to control my bleeding. He was very experienced and always cool as a cucumber, and he had a great sense of humor. During my years of infertility, he and I had become close. He seemed to adore Tim and me, and we felt he treated us like family. He even came early to the hospital that day to shoot the breeze and talk hunting with my father before they wheeled me in.

As he was working on me, I remember saying something funny to him. When he didn't respond, I knew immediately that something was not right. He was very serious and focused. He had an intern doctor with him, but Dr. Torhorst took over abruptly. I never quite knew the seriousness of my blood loss until one day, several months later, he mentioned how he was busy trying to save my life. He wanted us to have this baby as much as Tim and I did, and he did everything to have it all work out.

During the C-section, even with the craziness, my doctor checked out my reproductive organs. He noticed my one fallopian tube was "kinked," and was held down by some scar tissue. He clipped the scar tissue, and my tube went right back into position. After our baby was born, he commented that he wouldn't be surprised if we became pregnant on our own now.

Our beautiful daughter was born on a gorgeous day in October. We chose her first name to be Kianna, which means "strength." Her middle name, Verdell, was chosen after my grandmother, the one who died when I was nineteen. Since I was very close to my grandmother, it meant the world to me for Kianna to have my grandmother's name. Tim didn't dispute it for a second, as he knew how much it meant to me.

It was my grandmother who got me hooked on dolls when I was a child. She bought me a baby doll or collectible doll each Christmas. I still remember the excitement I felt when I opened up my two special baby dolls, each in different years. I still have them. Their names are Angela and Sabrina. They've had a lot of use. My grandmother showed me just what to do with my "baby"—how to hold it, feed it, and change it. All pretend fun. One year she crocheted a beautiful, yellow blanket with animals on it for my dolls. She told me to hang on to it for my own real baby some day. I did. I still have it today, and it has had a *lot* of use.

My parents were wonderful through it all and helped us to adjust to our precious miracle baby. I was completely ecstatic. Even when she'd wake at night, I was thrilled to go to her, just to be with her.

October 9, 1995

Today is the day—we did the amnio this morning and are now awaiting the results to see if the baby's lungs are developed. I'm a bit shaky—I feel like I had caffeine this morning. The amnio went fine. It hurt a little bit, but it didn't poke the baby. I am so happy. I can't believe everything that is happening.

If the lungs are developed, we will be parents today!

October 14, 1995

Our dream came true on October 9, 1995, at 6:32 p.m. Our beautiful daughter was born. Kianna Verdell Hanson.

She is the most beautiful sight I've ever seen, and I love her more than I ever thought humanly possible. I don't have a lot of time right now. I just finished nursing her, and I have the pillow the length of my legs, and she's lying facing me.

She's really gorgeous! So adorable and such a miracle!

November 9, 1995

Our little peanut is sleeping right now, so I thought I'd write. She's incredible. The way she cries when she is hungry and how she gets so impatient. The way she gets all excited when she's going after my breast to feed, and the satisfied, smug look on her little face when she's filled her belly. Then she looks at me and smiles with such a contented look. When she's in her alert mode, she opens her eyes so wide and looks around, and she puckers her little lips. The way she likes to put her arms up in the air when she sleeps . . .

She makes my heart melt. I see her personality develop more every day. She's so sweet. When I hold her over my shoulder and feel her soft hair against my cheek and how she bobs her head around and practically kisses my cheek; the way she kicks so strongly when she wants to stretch out. I love her so much. Tim and I are so happy.

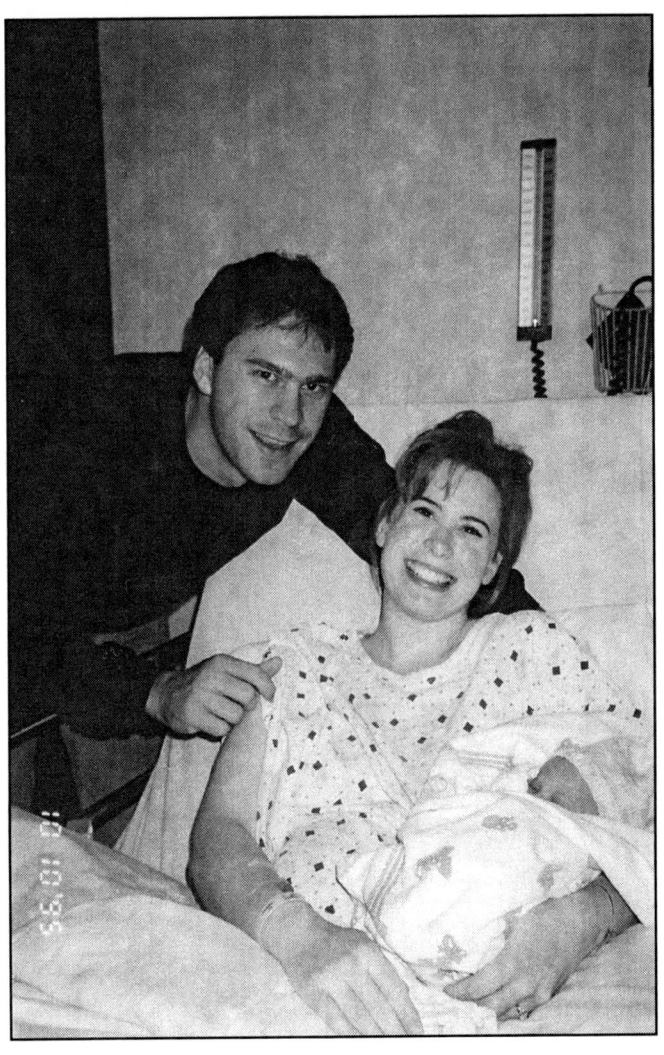

Proud first time parents

CHAPTER 8

STAYING FOCUSED
ON THE POSITIVE

OUR LIFE AFTER Kianna was born seemed like heaven on earth. She was our life, and she was an incredible child. I continued to work with a flexible schedule and eventually negotiated to reduce my hours so I could be home with her more often.

Dr. Torhorst told me we should try to get pregnant again before my endometriosis made its comeback. We did everything we could, but it was not happening.

I finally did conceive naturally. It is not written here with the excitement you would expect because it sadly ended in miscarriage. It was a tough time.

Prior to this, Dr. Torhorst had been diagnosed with cancer. The last time I saw him, he was joking around with me and his nurse Diane about how we'd talk about him when he was gone. He had lost his hair due to his chemotherapy treatments, and we told him he was just as handsome without hair. When I found out I was pregnant, I called Dr. Torhorst's office and learned he had taken a turn for the worse. He had only a short time to live. It was very sad. How ironic that Dr. Torhorst had been our cheerleader through all of our struggles and took such a personal interest in making our dreams come true. Now, as we were celebrating our new-found joy of life with Kianna and possibly expecting another, his life was coming to an end. It really brought into perspective how precious life is.

I was struggling. While I needed to see a doctor, it was difficult to go to someone else. Part of me felt like I was somehow betraying Dr. Torhorst, like I had used him for what we wanted, and now I was going to simply move on to another doctor who could help us. Finally, realizing I had no choice, I followed up with the doctor who had helped us with our IVF through University of Wisconsin Hospital.

June 16, 1997

Well, a lot has happened since I wrote last. I'm apparently pregnant. We are not sure if we are out of the woods. I just received my second HCG test, and they are concerned that the levels are not going up fast enough. Yes, I did say pregnant—we had a confirmed positive test, but now we have to go back tomorrow to meet with the doctor because the levels are not where they should be. I'm a little nervous, but God will take care of everything. I have no control, and I need to remember that. I would be amazed if I did become pregnant; it would be a miracle.

June 21, 1997

The HCG levels are still not where they need to be. The doctor said I'm going to miscarry. I'm OK one minute and ready to bawl the next. All in all I know I have Kianna and Tim, and that's all I could ever ask for. That is all I ever did really ask for, and God gave that to me.

It's just hard. I have all the symptoms of being pregnant (6–7 weeks) but know that the baby is not making it. I'm even getting a belly. It's all so emotional. But we know I can get pregnant; we just need help with the hormones next time.

Dr. Torhorst is dying. I'm upset about that too. I miss him so much. I don't trust the other doctor as much. Dr. Torhorst is my friend. He's got cancer. He delivered Kianna and was there through everything while Tim and I were trying to get pregnant. I can't believe he's only got a few days to live. I remember all of our talks.

We continued to wait as we also waited for news on Dr. Torhorst. I soon learned he passed away. He left behind his loving family. He was a charismatic man with a great smile, and it was hard to believe he was gone. I thought about all of the time he spent with Tim and me. He cared so much for us and all of his patients. He was so full of life.

Prior to his death, when he joked about how much we'd miss him when he was gone, we grew quiet. None of us wanted to hear him talk like that. We'd tell him he'd fight it, although part of me knew he wasn't so sure. At one point, he asked me something that now, looking back, is starting to make sense. He asked if I could write something to him about how he helped me. Maybe he knew of his pending death and wanted to reflect back on his life. While I wondered about the request, I was very willing to write it. Since a lot of our discussions and time together were often light-hearted, it was difficult for either of us to know what to say when he received my letter that described how much he had helped us. In fact, he did joke that he wanted me to remember this when he was dead. He said it in such a matter-of-fact way that it was hard to really know if he was serious. I preferred to ignore the possibility.

Due to my health challenges over the years, I had to see Dr. Torhorst monthly. I also knew I had the "thickest" file of all of his patients. Based upon our last conversation, I asked to speak at the funeral to represent his patients. His wife agreed. When I stood in front of hundreds of people, inside me was a pregnancy I was waiting to lose. As I looked around the church and saw so many people, I realized how many lives he had impacted. It was hard to believe he was really gone.

July 11, 1997

Dr. Torhorst died. I spoke at his funeral. I miss him. It was always a comfort knowing he was there for me at all times. Now he's not. My heart breaks for his wife, Cheryl, and his children. He really loved life.

I'm still pregnant. We don't know for sure if everything is OK or not. The HCG level was much higher than expected today. I had an ultrasound, and the doctor said he might have seen something in the sac, but he couldn't be sure. I have another HCG Sunday and an ultrasound Monday. Hopefully we'll know more.

A couple of days after the funeral, I went back to see the doctor. He said the baby should "pass" on its own, but it still hung in there. We continued to wait until we finally confirmed that there was no sign of life inside me, then scheduled a D&C. This is when the lining of the uterus is scraped to empty its contents should the fetus not pass on its own.

This was one of the most difficult experiences of my life. I have never felt more violated. While I encountered many wonderful doctors, nurses and staff, I did have one horrible nurse.

Having a D&C is emotional and hard enough under any circumstance, but the insensitivity of one of the nurses who prepped me for the procedure was unbelievable. Rather than treating me gently, she was gruff and physically rough. They gave me Valium, and she proceeded to insert something into me that looked like a "sponge on a stick," perhaps with iodine solution on it. She jammed it in me, if you know what I mean.

By this point, with several past surgeries and endometriosis, I knew what was normal, and I had experience with pain. I had a high pain tolerance. When this woman did this, I jumped and said, "Oh, I'm sorry, but that really hurt!" I tried to say it as kindly as I could. However, in hindsight, I should have (and very much felt like) kicking her as hard as I could in the mouth to defend myself. What happened next I am still livid about. She said, "This one's a jumper!" Next thing I knew, they knocked me completely out. I felt violated—almost as if I were raped. I had no control over the situation.

To this day, I regret not following up and sending a letter to the hospital about the nurse's actions. It still makes my blood boil as I picture this large, rough, gruff woman.

After the procedure, I bled significantly for two or three weeks. I called the doctor's office, only to be assured this was normal. In my teenage years, I had experience with extremely heavy periods, but this was *much* worse. Tim and I went camping for a few days with Kianna, and I constantly had to go the restroom to take care of things. I continually felt faint from blood loss. Eventually the bleeding stopped, but I felt that perhaps they had scraped too deep and caused my significant bleeding.

After the D&C, time continued without a successful pregnancy. It was recommended that we try IVF again. We got on the waiting list and went through the process.

This time it was a complete flop. My eggs took awhile to fertilize, and when they did, they were not of "good quality." They said they could implant them and they might take off, or they could just let nature take its course, and we could see how things evolved. They didn't. The doctors were confused and told us this had not happened in many years. A pregnancy might not occur, but the eggs almost always fertilize properly. It was strange; it was as if I was just going through the motions this time around. My heart never felt connected to the process. I could not quite explain it.

As if this wasn't difficult enough, the doctor nicked my bladder during the retrieval. I was unable to go to the bathroom because my bladder was plugged with blood clots. When I called the doctor, he assured me it was not coming from the bladder, but from my uterus. I assured *them* I knew my body, and it was *not* coming from my uterus.

They told me to come in (for them to prove it was not my bladder). After they checked me over, *I* was right; *they* were wrong. Of course.

Dr. Torhorst always took my word for things. We had the kind of relationship where he was aware that I knew my body and was always very informed. He never second-guessed me. I missed Dr. Torhorst all over again. Somehow, I got over this as well.

November 5, 1998

It's over. None of the embryos continued to grow, so we never went to the transfer stage. When we received the call Monday, the doctor said it was over, but he continued to watch the embryos to make sure. Tuesday, same thing. They said they checked on their end, and nothing was done wrong. They checked the "matter" they were fertilized in, and all the other couples who used the same matter had no problem with it. We need to decide if we want to do it again. They said they could get us in February.

We need to think about it. God needs to help us with the decision.

Since this IVF attempt failed, we would have to start again on the waiting list for another round. However, the doctor said that under the circumstances, they would try to move us closer to the top of the list.

Meanwhile, as we were waiting for the call that they were ready for us, I got an important call from Jennifer.

It's amazing (as is much that you have already read and will read in my book), but over the phone she told me, "God told me to tell you that he let you do it your way with Kianna, but now he wants to do it his way."

Wow! Talk about really putting it out there. I was in a daze. Here I was, finally "getting" what it meant to trust God, and here was a blatant statement I needed to listen to. If this came from anyone else, I may have thought, "Yeah, but she just doesn't get it." But, this was Jennifer. She did "get it." What was interesting, though, is that throughout this time I remember feeling as though we would have more children, but I didn't get the sense there was a connection to IVF. It was kind of the same feeling I got back when we tried IVF the very first time, when deep down I knew I didn't have God's blessing. This time; however, I knew better than to ignore this feeling. This feeling, combined with Jennifer's message from God (I will still never quite know how this message came to her, she is always so amazing), was enough for me to change direction. It's like I was taking a leap and just waited to see how it would turn out. Kind of scary, yes. Kind of exciting, too.

I shared Jennifer's message with Tim. He and I never had many deep philosophical or religious discussions, so he just listened and kind of said, "Whatever." Not in a sarcastic way, but like he didn't quite understand but would go along with what I wanted. He also knew that since this was my body going through it, I was the one who needed to be OK with the decision.

Shortly after Jennifer's call, the doctor's office called to tell us we were "up." Quite honestly, I was not 100% sure how I would respond when the call came. Part of me assumed I would put them off and let them know I'd get back to them and prolong it a bit more. When it was time for me to respond, it was like a new-found confidence and courage came over me. I heard myself tell them we were not going to move ahead with it this time.

Despite everything we had been going through with the miscarriage and failed attempts for another pregnancy and the death of my doctor, I remained thankful for our healthy daughter and grateful for my husband. I really was *so* fulfilled. I prayed to God to surprise me. I also knew every day is a gift from God. This was reinforced in my mind with the death of Dr. Torhorst. I kept his family in my prayers.

CHAPTER 9

WHEN YOU LET HIM DO IT HIS WAY, THINGS HAPPEN

January 27, 1999

Kianna and I are home today. I have walking pneumonia, and she has pink eye.

Not a lot new except Sue is in the process of adopting a baby and the friend I've been "counseling" is pregnant!

Kianna is precious. Things are great. We are going to Maui in March, and I can't wait. I'm trying to get into shape.

February 2, 1999

It's official! Sue and Chris are parents! They have the baby in their home tonight. I'm so happy for them. They will be wonderful parents. She asked me to be Hope's godmother. I'm honored.

I pray for Annie and Bob now. I can't help but worry that she's been forgotten. God, please let a miracle happen for them with a baby very soon. Please let them find a baby to adopt, and help them to focus on going in the right direction.

I also pray that Tim and I will conceive in Hawaii, that the timing would be perfect, and that I give birth to another healthy child 9 months later. God, I pray that the world continues to grow with people who believe in you. I wish I could do more to help so the world becomes more as it should be in the way you created it. Please help me to walk in the direction you want me to go, and please help my husband to walk in the same direction to support me. I know I want to be a Stephen Minister some day (this is a program through the church that helps minister to people in need), but I want to do more. Please help me to do more.

Tim, Kianna, and I planned to take a vacation in March of 1999 to Maui, Hawaii. It was fun to travel, and Kianna was easy to take along. We certainly could not leave her behind, and we welcomed the opportunity to spend some quality, family time together.

Quality family time, however, was going to have to wait, as it proved to be a long trip to Maui. The day started off on the wrong foot. We awoke at 5:00 a.m. to several inches of snow. When we got to the airport, we learned our initial flight was delayed several hours, until 1:00 p.m. This would give us less than thirty minutes in Minneapolis to catch the flight to Honolulu.

Waiting for our flight at the Madison airport, we tried to remain patient and entertained Kianna. We eventually departed Madison, arrived in Minneapolis, rushed to our gate, and got there just in time to catch the flight to Honolulu. We had an eight-hour flight, and then we would catch another quick flight to Maui.

Throughout the morning and on the airplane, Kianna was a bit "off," and her tummy bothered her for the entire trip. After frequent trips to the plane's restroom, she continued to be uncomfortable. Eventually, she fell asleep and slept for a large portion of the flight to Honolulu. She slept again as we switched planes for the short flight to Maui.

Finally on the ground in Maui, Kianna was too tired to walk, so she asked Daddy to carry her through the airport. She had one last surprise for Tim. She got sick as we were heading to the baggage claim—all over Daddy and the escalator! What a mess. Tim retrieved our luggage, changed into a clean shirt, got the rental car and directions to the hotel, and got us on the road. At 1:30 a.m. we finally collapsed into our room at the hotel. After more than twenty hours of travel, weather delays, three different flights, and a sick kid, we were exhausted. Kianna, on the other hand, had other things in mind. She had slept most of the flight and now felt much better after her episode at the airport. She was ready and raring to go. This was paradise? What kind of vacation were we in for?

Well, as it turned out, Maui *was* paradise. It was incredibly relaxing. We hung out at the beach, relaxed by the pool, and took in some of the most beautiful natural scenery in the world. We went on a whale watch and attended a luau pig roast, complete with the hula girls in the grass skirts. Kianna and Tim even joined them on stage. We had a blast.

On our last night in Maui, we returned to the hotel lobby from dinner to experience one of the most memorable moments of our lives. Soft, Hawaiian music filled the open-air lounge, accompanied by the most amazing, calming voice. A fresh, cool breeze from the ocean brought the wonderful aroma of salt water and coconut trees. Tim and I breathed deeply and closed our eyes as we listened to Jamie Lawrence sing "Maui Waltz." We bought a CD to recapture the experience back home. To this day, we listen to the CD, relax, close our eyes, and remember what a wonderful experience God created for us.

March 26, 1999

It's Friday night. Kianna and I were playing "sharks." I was the mommy shark and she was the baby shark. Tim and Kianna were playing "bears" before. She's such an incredible child. She has a great laugh and an absolutely wonderful smile that lights up the world. We are so blessed.

We went to Maui—it was great. Really relaxing. We went to a luau where Tim and Kianna were chosen to go on stage to learn how to hula. We sat with a fun group of people. We went on a whale watch and took a drive to the mountains to Hana. It's beautiful there!

Tania (friend of the family) had her twin boys. She will be a great mommy. Paula (good friend) is due any day—April 1. I'm excited for them. Jennifer's mom needs a kidney transplant, and Jen wants to donate one if hers is a match. I pray God will heal Jackie and that if Jen does donate that she'll be OK. How very difficult.

I'm thinking we might try IVF again. I was wondering if we needed to wait—if God was going to make it happen naturally, but I have not had any signs or feelings one way or another. I pray for guidance. I also wonder what my body is up to. I feel so bloated lately and wonder if I ovulated or not. I get frustrated with my body, but it's better than it was with my endo at least. I keep having this feeling that I'll be getting cancer some day and that I won't live to be old. The thought of leaving Kianna and Tim is heartbreaking. I wonder if I'm worrying over nothing, or if I'm predicting my own fate. I pray God keeps me healthy and helps me to live to be old. Tim and Kianna too, of course. Life is hard. What's helped me is my faith, and I could stand to spend more time with it. I try to witness to others and touch others, but I get inundated with so many things that I tend not to take time to really talk and listen to God.

Once home, I started to realize little changes with my body. I was confused and worried. My body seemed to be "off," and soon I was dealing with one thing after another. My temperature had increased slightly, but I also discovered I had a urinary tract infection. After receiving treatment for it, I got my first yeast infection. I learned this is common when on antibiotics. I was busy dealing with all of this when I realized I was also late starting my next cycle.

I didn't think it possible, but I got a pregnancy test anyway. Wouldn't hurt, right? I was shocked that after everything, I was pregnant! Tim couldn't believe it. After all of our attempts, it happened naturally. We didn't want to get our hopes up too much, however, considering my last miscarriage. In my heart, though, I thought it was too perfect.

April 9, 1999

I'm pregnant. We conceived in Maui! All by ourselves. I have all the symptoms this time. There was a reason I chose not to do in vitro again. We had the first levels done, and they were good. I go for an ultrasound tomorrow. I can't believe it! I'm so happy. I feel peace that everything will be OK this time.

April 11, 1999

The 2nd levels were great! Thank the wonderful Lord! It's amazing. We waited on IVF, and look what happened. God came through without delay, although after an interesting month, I didn't think it was possible.

My first plan was to call the IVF doctor's office. It was quite a shock to their staff considering they had just called me, offering a spot with their last IVF round. They scheduled an ultrasound and found a healthy baby. I was six weeks pregnant. We were on "cloud nine."

They told me I "graduated" into a normal OB/GYN office since I had conceived naturally and the baby was doing well. I was not sure where to turn since the death of Dr. Torhorst. I found out that Diane, the nurse that worked with Dr. Torhorst, went with another OB/GYN group, so I called her.

Diane recommended I see a female doctor with the group, Dr. Julie Schurr, because she thought our personalities would mesh. She was right. We hit it off immediately, and I really appreciated Dr. Schurr's professionalism and attentiveness. She explained things well and made me feel taken care of.

She decided she wanted to schedule another ultrasound to take a look at how things were progressing. Due to my past challenge with placenta previa, she wanted to determine the location of my placenta. During the ultrasound appointment (I was eight weeks by this time), the ultrasound technician seemed to be taking a long time. As I watched her looking carefully at everything, I also noticed another blackened area on the ultrasound screen. I started to wonder, and to worry at the same time.

The woman finally pointed out that she saw *two* babies. Tim and I were in shock! She also mentioned concerns. Baby A was growing well and was the size it should be at eight weeks. The amniotic fluid and size of the sac around the baby were great. Baby B, however, was about two weeks smaller in size for an eight-week pregnancy, and the sac around her contained a very low level of amniotic fluid. She was concerned Baby

B might not survive. My head was spinning as she continued to mention Baby A and Baby B. We still did not have our heads around the concept of twins, yet the concerns did not leave us any time to grasp all that was happening.

As she went out to get a doctor to consult with us, I watched both babies moving around on the screen. They were so tiny, yet I could already see their heads, bodies, and limbs. I already knew I had fallen in love with *both* of them. They were alive, and they were in my womb. I was afraid and happy at the same time. With everything in me, I wanted both of them to survive. I was determined to ensure the babies would be safe.

Tim was concerned and did not want to get his hopes up—or see my hopes become crushed. As we spoke to the doctor (Dr. Schurr was not there at that time, so we talked to her colleague), he gently explained the typical scenario. He explained that it was likely Baby B would not survive. He told us that although it was hard to tell, I should not be alarmed if I started to hemorrhage if the baby miscarried. He also said it is possible the baby would be absorbed back into my body, and that the other baby should not be affected.

We had to wait a long month before we knew what the future held for our little Baby B. It was a long month. We didn't tell many people about our situation, as it would be too difficult to tell people if one did not make it. Many knew we were expecting, but few knew what we were facing. It was a difficult time. If I let myself, I would have become overwhelmed with the situation. I couldn't handle it. Once again, I had to remember that God was with us, and if I trusted him, he would get me through this.

Jennifer was the only person who really believed with all of her heart that both babies would make it and that I was having twins. I prayed hard that she was right. I loved them both and wanted to bring them into the world. They were my babies. My mother-instinct wanted to protect them—no matter what.

During this, Jennifer called me at work and said she had a dream of two children. She believed they were twins, walking along the beach and holding hands. She said she could not remember if they were girls or boys, but she remembered one seemed a little smaller than the other. At the time, I didn't think much about it, but I thought it did offer some hope.

May 1, 1999

I'm carrying twins! The only thing is, the sac around one baby is quite small. That's a concern. I pray they will both be OK. They both had strong heartbeats. One was about 2 weeks smaller than the other. I'm hoping they just couldn't get the right angle to see the rest of the sac. We go in again on the 24th, so we need to wait and see. I know God will take care of us. Jennifer is convinced both babies will be OK. It's a miracle. We did IVF 3 times. One time it worked with Kianna, and on our own God gives us twins. Not on our own, with God taking over. He's showing us just how powerful he is. It's incredible. I've been sick to my stomach, mostly in the AM and into early afternoon, but it's not bad. My belly is filling out. My jeans do not fit.

I had lunch yesterday with a motivational speaker. He's interested in my joining his organization in the future. I would like to someday, but with twins, however, there really is no way I'll be able to work for a while—until they are at least 2. Then they can go to Preschool of the Arts. I can't see having 3 children in daycare at the same time. It will be difficult for me personally also. When they are little I'd like to have them with me. If they were in day care, they would be sick a lot. I am the one who needs to be available to pick them up from school and take them home since Tim's job demands travel, etc. I always need to be the "back-up." I can't do that with 3 children and work at the level I need to, to be successful. If I were to join the new organization, it would be flexible, but as far as income is concerned, since it is a growing company, it would be purely pay for performance.

May 2, 1999

We told Dean about the babies. He cried. He's so sweet. Tim and I are beginning to get excited about the twins. We've been concerned about them, so we were afraid to say much. I know it will be a lot of work—but worth it! I've been thinking about the logistics of twins. How will I do this and that, etc. Then I realize I'll need to do everything with a double stroller, with car/carrier seats that fit into the stroller. I'm excited about it. We'll have to make sure Kianna does not feel left out or jealous. Although I'm not so naïve to think it won't happen. We'll have to focus extra attention for her. I think Tim is warming up to my not working if the twins are both OK. What a relief! I would be crazy to think I could work with twins. It's difficult enough with one.

Our one-month wait finally passed, and we were on pins and needles during the next ultrasound. What a miracle! The doctor found two babies once again! This time they were both bigger and wiggling all over. I was ecstatic, and I think Tim was in (happy) shock. It was amazing! We were really pregnant with twins. We were tickled watching them together on the ultrasound screen. They'd kick each other in the head and looked like they were having a blast together.

Baby B was still measured about two weeks smaller than his/her twin, but the level of amniotic fluid had improved. The doctors assumed the twins were fraternal, due to the size difference, and thought maybe they just took after different sides of the family. They did say they wanted to monitor the situation closely to make sure each baby grew according to her own growth chart.

Every few weeks, we had another ultrasound to monitor their growth. They were concerned about twin-to-twin transfusion, when the blood from one baby is taken from the other. They also classified them as having a "discordance in size."

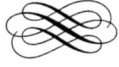

May 26, 1999

12 weeks, 1 day

The babies are doing well! We had our ultrasound on Monday, and they were wiggling around, moving their little arms and legs. It was incredible. The smaller one is catching up and the sac is also.

Annie's adoption looks like it is going through! What a wonderful God we have! I'm so happy for them.

My boss also told the General Manager. He congratulated me and said we'll talk when I'm ready. He was warm about it.

June 1, 1999

13 weeks

I felt the babies kick last night—just a wham right under by belly button. It's so incredible. I feel very big tonight. Tim and I went to dinner at Otto's. Kianna does not have school this week, so she's staying two nights with Grandma and Grandpa. That's the first time she's been away for more than one night. I really miss her. She's having fun, though. She's been riding a horse! She's so wonderful.

About three months into the pregnancy, I was so exhausted that I couldn't walk across a room without feeling like I was going to collapse. I asked the doctor about it, and she confirmed that I was anemic and put me on a high dose of iron supplements. Further testing revealed I had a borderline thyroid problem. I remember being so hungry and having certain cravings, but I was too tired to go to the grocery store to buy food. Tim had to step in and tried to accommodate.

The iron helped, but the pregnancy was very challenging to my body. I was out of breath all the time; I also felt my heart pumping extra hard trying to sustain and meet the needs of the twins. How in the world do women with more do it?

Gaining weight turned out to be a struggle, as well. I felt like I was starving *all* the time, yet when I got food, I could only eat a small amount due to the twins taking up a lot of space in my abdomen. I could almost feel the twins yanking on the umbilical cord, yelling for me to bring down more food. It was funny. I'd imagine them pleading for food, then when they got fed, they were "groov'n" big time and would move around like they were at a party. My favorite pig-out craving was a big Culver's cheeseburger. When I was still working, my coworkers never argued about where we'd go for lunch—they knew never to argue with a pregnant mother of twins. They'd try to get me to finish my burger (I usually had a thick shake too), but I couldn't.

Even though I was not as big as one would expect for being pregnant with twins, Tim and Kianna thought it great fun to tease me. As I got bigger, I "waddled," and they came up with my new nickname, "Jumbolia." One night we went to a restaurant for dinner, and Kianna walked behind me, mimicking me and how I walked. I became suspicious when I heard people snickering as we walked by. When I caught her, she and Tim laughed their heads off.

Towards the end of my pregnancy, my dear friends threw a wonderful twin baby shower. I knew that traditionally, you only have a shower for your first baby, but my friends/coworkers really wanted to do something for me. They knew that with twins, I'd need two of everything, and they discussed my new needs with me. The bigger goal was to have a party to celebrate their coming birth. Knowing I'm what they called a "tea and crumpet" kind of gal, my loving friends planned just that. In fact, they called it a "Tea for two" party. Gail, Annie, Sara, Milissa, Mary, and other friends planned and prepared for it. It was absolutely lovely. I was touched by their effort and their understanding of what kind of party I would appreciate. The party was held at Gail's house. Annie, Gail, Sara, Milissa, and others all pitched in with various teas and pastries/crumpets. They decorated the table with fine china and flowers. As someone who finds it difficult to "receive," I was overwhelmed with gratitude.

A few months into the pregnancy, the lease for my vehicle was coming due. We needed to choose a new vehicle that would accommodate a family of five (with three car seats). We went back and forth between mini vans and a bigger SUV, such as a Suburban. We knew Suburbans did not have the best gas mileage. While we were conscious of the environment, Tim was very adamant about safety. He believed safety was #1. I agreed. While I was still trying to decide (since I loved the many kid-friendly options of the mini vans), something happened that confirmed my decision. A horrible accident in Middleton that resulted in the death of two children occurred. A family was on their way home from church when a drunk driver going forty-five miles per hour hit the side of their mini van, killing their two children. It was horrific, and I felt so bad for the parents. I could not imagine the depth of pain they were in. Mini vans are very safe for most accident situations, but as I had prayed for guidance, I felt as though we were being led to go for the bigger, safer vehicle.

Toward the end of the pregnancy, I was on bed rest, or so the doctors thought. I remembered being told, "Take it easy." *That was easy for them to say*, I thought. I have a job and a three-year-old to care for. My next appointment confirmed that I must be on full bed rest for the remainder of my pregnancy. I was glad; my body was having a hard time. One day, shortly before I was on complete bed rest, I had to sit down three times as I walked Kianna from the car into the pre-school, because I kept feeling faint. It was embarrassing. There was no place to sit, so I sat down on the curb, very un-lady like, with my legs apart and my big belly hanging down, with Kianna asking, "What's wrong, Mommy?" As I tried to see through the stars, I was seeing, while covered in a cold sweat, I responded, "I'm OK, honey. Mommy just needs to sit down for a moment." A few more steps, same thing. Looking back, I realize how foolish I was not to ask for help. If a friend was in my shoes, I would have demanded she let me drive her home, and I'd call her husband and doctor. Not me, though. Oh no, I didn't want to bother anyone.

September 6, 1999

27 weeks

Well, as I start my 28th week, I'm as big as I was when I had Kianna. Starting this week, I'll be working from home. I had to cut back to ½ days at 24 weeks, but my body needs more rest. I had an ultrasound a week ago, and the babies are a ½ lb apart. There was some concern, and the doctor said it's important that I rest—and eat well.

I'm starting to phase out of work these days. On the one hand, I'm relieved; on the other hand, I'm not 100% ready to give up my clients. Tomorrow I need to work on a memo for my plan as to who will do what. We are almost set for the babies now! Just a few more odds and ends. The babies might be girls. They were chewing and had their arms up over their heads!

September 20, 1999

I start my 30th week tomorrow! I'm officially not working anymore as of today. I still need to make a couple of phone calls, but otherwise, I'm on leave. I still will get work calls, but in order to get paid the next two months, I guess I don't have a choice. It's tempting just to be done completely, since I still get budget questions. At least today I did.

I'm on bed rest, I guess. I can do very little. They are concerned about the one baby, and I start major testing this week to check everything. I'll go to St. Mary's for it.

Due to the twins' size difference, I had been going to a high-risk pregnancy doctor at St. Mary's Hospital. When I was thirty weeks pregnant, the doctor was pleased that the girls continued to grow at their own rates. Although Baby A continued to be bigger, they were still proportionate. She told me to come back in four weeks. At the last minute she changed her mind and said we should come back in three weeks instead.

That week made a significant difference.

When we went back three weeks later, we expected everything would, once again, go well. It was anything but. First the radiologist checked things out, and then the doctor came in as well. The mood was serious as they continued to review the ultrasound. My heart was pounding. Inside, I was paralyzed with fear. The doctor explained that the ultrasound indicated that Baby B had stopped growing since the last appointment. When they checked the umbilical cord to take a look at the blood flow, it indicated that the baby was getting roughly half of the flow it should be getting. It was a very serious situation; the baby was starving. It was not getting the proper nutrition through the placenta and cord. The babies needed to be born quickly.

We were scared. They told me the babies had to come out right away in order to save the smaller one's life. I remember being in shock as we walked down the hall. Rather than going home, I was to be admitted immediately into the hospital. I felt so out of control. No matter how hard I tried to ensure the babies would be born OK, I really had little control over what was happening inside of my body. I tried to shrug off the feeling that I somehow did something wrong to have things turn out this way. While my head knew that was crazy, I was disappointed with my body, that I couldn't do what needed to be done to ensure the babies' health.

We called my parents and asked them to pick up Kianna from pre-school that afternoon and explained the situation.

When we got to my hospital room, I was immediately hooked up to the monitors so they could evaluate the babies' heart rates. They told me they would give me a shot of steroids to help the babies' lungs develop more quickly; they told me even a day longer in my womb to allow this to happen would benefit the babies. They continued to monitor them around the clock and were ready to move quickly into the operating room if their heart rates dropped.

While it was a frightening situation, the doctors and nurses were wonderful. One of the doctors from the group I go to was there when we were admitted. He was kind and reassuring. He explained everything and sounded confident that everything would be OK. We were mostly concerned about the baby's organs—would the baby have any developmental issues? Would it lead a normal life? He took time to answer our questions and explained that in situations like this, the baby's body instinctively goes into "survival mode." It tells its body to mature faster, and it also gives the vital organs the greatest priority from the nutrition it does have. He said the limbs would get the least, and that was OK. They can always catch up after delivery.

He then went on to discuss the delivery. We had planned another C-section. Since Kianna was delivered via C-section, and since I was going to have twins, it would be best to go this route. This plan was determined by my regular doctor, but the doctor did not know this; therefore, he moved on as if it would be a regular delivery.

He discussed how they would induce me and explained how it should be fairly easy because they were little. After the larger one was born, the little one should have no problems coming. My head was spinning, as I had no plans to deliver normally. When he finished discussing it, I carefully mentioned the plans for C-section and hoped he was in agreement. He drew a big sigh of relief and admitted that a C-section would be a less stressful way to go, and he was happy to hear this.

I felt confident in what he was telling us and was grateful for his sensitivity to our situation. He was a father, too, and understood how we felt. He talked to us like we were friends with real feelings and real children.

After the doctor left, a nurse by the name of Lisa came in. Her job was to talk to us about what to expect the next day—providing the C-section was not moved up. She worked in the Neonatal Intensive Care Unit (NICU), and she took the time to talk to me and get to know me while she explained how the team of doctors would be ready for the babies and how anything they needed to ensure they received proper care would be fulfilled. She explained everything from if/when we could see the babies, to how long they might need to be there, to challenges preemie babies and their parents face. This included everything from eating issues, checking for congenital issues, and everything in between. She discussed how visiting works and how we needed to wash our hands for three minutes before we could go in, and who is allowed for visits.

It was scary, but she was reassuring and gentle as well. I appreciated her kindness and empathetic nature. We continued to talk about Kianna and what it would be like to have twins, as she sat on my bed. She was a great support.

I was as ready as I would ever be, I thought.

The next step was to get through the night. They had not let me eat or drink anything since I was admitted, because they didn't know when I'd need to be rushed in for the C-section, so my body was a bit dehydrated. With this came contractions. They were not severe, but were enough to keep me awake. Tim was there with me the entire time, and our challenge for the night was to keep the monitors in the right spots on my big belly. Every time one of the babies moved, the monitors had to be re-adjusted. We knew the importance of evaluating them every second, so we did whatever it took. We did know, however, that every time they moved, it was a good sign.

We made it until the next day. The babies hung in there. I was impressed and knew already they were strong and had the will to survive.

The time had come; the doctors did not want to wait any longer, so it was time to wheel me into the operating room. They had to give me a spinal. I still remember how uncomfortable and difficult it was for me to bend over to receive it. The doctor had a little difficulty, it seemed, getting it in just the right spot.

As with Kianna, they put up a little curtain shield so I would not be able to watch what was going on. A nurse held one hand, and Tim held the other as they started the procedure. There were many nurses and doctors ready to go.

It was quiet in the operating room, as everyone was full of anticipation. When the doctor took the first baby out, she let out a small cry. It was the sweetest music to my ears, but the mood quickly changed. It got quiet again as Baby B was lifted out of my body.

I could hear a bit of a gasp from nurses when they took out our second tiny girl. I didn't hear anything that time except maybe a snuffle. The silence was deafening. I hated not being able to see what was going on. I laid there asking, over and over, "Is the baby OK? Is the baby OK? What is going on?" Tim said quietly, "She's really small; they took her into the other room." The nurse told me in a reassuring voice that doctors were checking her out, and she'd get an update for me. I felt so helpless. As I lay there, I continued to ask Tim to find out what was going on.

I knew there was little chance of holding the babies, yet my arms still felt . . . so . . . empty.

Soon the nurse and Tim reported she was doing OK, but she needed to be taken to the NICU to be cared for. The nurse did, however, tell me that our bigger twin was getting cleaned up and that I could hold her. I was ecstatic to connect with her outside of the womb. She was amazing. She was precious and so tiny. It seemed unreal that she could be so perfect yet so small. Although I could not hold her very comfortably since the shield was still up and the doctors were attempting to close me up, it felt good to feel her warm little body next to me.

While I was holding her, one of the nurses showed me both of the umbilical cords. The bigger twin's was a normal size and looked healthy, but seeing the other one took my breath away. It was shrunken and looked dried up. It was sad to think of my baby struggling to stay alive, with little nutrition going through an umbilical cord half the normal size. It was a miracle she was still alive!

As I held the larger twin, the nurses realized that she was struggling to breathe. She needed to go to the NICU for observation and to be properly cared for. They told me they would bring the other baby's isolate into the hallway when I was transferred into the recovery room so I could peek in on her. The head nurse, also named Diane, admitted her. When I finally saw our tiny baby, I just stared at her in awe. I wanted so badly to reach in and hold her and let her know I was there and how much I loved her. I wanted to love her and protect her and make her all better. It was difficult to be separated from her through the isolate. It was great though, that the nurse told us she was a little pistol, and she was doing amazingly well. Even her lungs were fully developed. She was 2 lbs., 14 ounces. Her "big" sister was 4 lbs., 12 ounces.

We decided on the name Natania for our smaller twin, "a gift from God." The bigger twin we named Brialle, "strong one." We had it all planned out over the last twenty-four hours during the time we waited in the hospital prior to their birth. We decided Natania's middle name would be Jennifer (after the one who knew she would come into this world!), and we chose Brialle's middle name to be Angeline, after my paternal grandmother.

I was so delighted and loved how Nurse Diane described our little baby—she's a pistol, she's a fighter. . . . I clung to those words.

Nurse Diane was right about Natania being a pistol. She wiggling all over in the isolate and even managed to wiggle herself to one end. She knew what she was doing!

Soon we learned that the bigger twin, Brialle, continued to have respiratory problems. The concern quickly went to her. She had to be put on the ventilator. The nurses and doctors reassured us she would be fine and gently explained exactly what was going on, what wire was for what, why she had small tubes/wires going into her belly button, why she needed IV's, etc. They acted like things would be fine and cared for her as necessary. She looked so small and helpless! I wanted so badly to hold her in my arms.

When we checked in on Natania, it was amazing how little she was. Her skin was practically transparent. We could see movement in her chest as her heart beat. Her feet were so tiny, and her little hands and long fingers were slender, yet so perfect. It was amazing, that despite their small size, they had all of their fingers and teeny toes, hair on their head, and such perfect features on their faces.

The girls were on different sides of the NICU, based upon the level of care needed. Brialle's classification was greater for the moment because she was on a ventilator. We went from baby to baby, and often split up so each would have a parent with her the entire time we were allowed to visit.

Each visit started by washing our hands for exactly three minutes with a soap I will never forget the scent of. We sang to them and watched them breathe, and reached into their isolate to let them wrap their little hand around our pinkies. That was our only contact with them at first. I remember when "big sister" Kianna visited them and sang "Bye, bye, Miss American Pie" to her tiny sisters (this was the first song Daddy taught her when she started talking. It was precious).

Seeing all of the babies there was difficult; some were worse off than others. Some of the babies had been there for a very long time, and their parents were veterans, while others were only under close observation for a few days, knowing they were going home soon.

The doctors and nurses continued to carefully monitor our sweet babes. Things changed quickly, however. After the doctors did their rounds the next morning, the NICU doctor explained to me that they had heard a heart murmur in Natania's heart.

She explained to us how there is a small blood vessel that is open in the baby's heart, which closes within a few days of birth. Based on this, it is not uncommon for preemies to have murmurs. She then told us that they would have a pediatric cardiologist check her out just to play it safe. So far, everything they said seemed fairly common, so I did not let myself worry.

That evening, pediatric cardiologist, Dr. Weinhaus, greeted us. He explained that he wanted to discuss some findings on the echocardiogram he performed on Natania. He had such a calm, steady way about him, yet his eyes told me that what he was about to share was not good news.

Since I had just had a C-section that day before, I was being wheeled around in a wheelchair, so the doctor acknowledged I might need to rest and asked if we'd like to talk in my hospital room. We agreed. We had no idea what to expect. He explained some issues Natania was facing related to her heart. I was serious and asked if I could take notes so I could be clear on what he was saying. Although I was still on strong painkillers, I remember being crystal clear to be sure I understood everything he told us.

He carefully explained that Natania's more serious issues included a narrowing of her aorta, called a coarctation, as well as a significant hole in her heart (Venticular Septal Defect or VSD). There were a few other, less serious, issues I don't recall all the specifics of, but these were the ones that needed immediate attention.

As he talked, I took notes. Between my tears, I continued writing and asking questions. I remember it was as if my spirit was carrying on away from my body, as if I was not able to directly handle what was being discussed. We were numb.

The doctor continued to explain that Natania was doing fine at the moment, because the vessel leading from her heart (the "ductus arteriosus") had not closed yet and was carrying blood past the coarctation. A coarctation means that the aorta is narrow at one spot, and blood cannot flow to the rest of the body. He said that in the next two or three days, the vessel would close. When that happened, Natania's health would plummet, and she would go down hill fast. The only treatment was surgery to repair the coarctation. The doctor was not sure whether the VSD needed to be repaired immediately or whether it was too risky due to her size.

In the meantime, the doctors were going to give Natania medication that essentially made the body think it was back in the uterus. This would keep the blood vessel open that was keeping her alive until they could perform the surgery. The doctor assured us that they would be ready when the time came to give her the special medication, and he also advised us to have her transferred to another hospital, Children's Hospital of Wisconsin in Milwaukee, for surgery.

He shared with us that at that time, Children's Hospital would have the best care for a baby that small. There were doctors in Madison who performed heart surgeries, but they did not have an established program for pediatrics and especially for premies like Natania. He told us he was advising us based upon what he would want if she were his baby. We appreciated his honesty, and we did not question him.

Dr. Weinhaus was patient and understanding with us. He talked to us for a long time, late into the night, and answered all of our questions. When it was time for him to go, Tim and I were emotionally drained. We were shaken and scared, but we agreed we needed to get through one step at a time, and we would get through it together with God's help.

We didn't know when things would start happening with Natania. It was a waiting game; we knew soon she would be fighting for her life. We had to be prepared.

That night I experienced a great inner struggle. My body was anxious and confused. Since they had taken the babies before my body wanted to let them go, it was as if my body was not in-line with reality. I was also a mixed mess of emotion, with my hormones all out of whack. My instincts as a mother were to hold, feed, and care for my babies, yet I was not even given the opportunity to bond with them. My arms and heart ached for my babies.

My sleep was interrupted; I remember feeling extremely restless and anxious. I continued to experience the feeling of loss, in terms of something wonderful and joyous had been torn away from me. Reality of the situation ripped my body and mind from what every mother desires and physically needs. My body was screaming to breastfeed my babies as my milk started to come in. But there were no babies ready to be fed.

A nurse told me someone who represents a breast pump company would be visiting with me soon. Sure enough, a nice, but direct young woman came in and told me I needed a double breast pump. I kind of liked her style. I was an emotional mess, but she was so matter of fact about it and also gave me a great reason as to why my babies needed me and what I could do for them. She explained that the best thing I could do for my babies was to feed them the best and the most important nutrients through my breast milk. They called it liquid gold.

I was helpless, yet I was determined to take this job seriously. We talked about how they may not be able to take my breast milk yet, but they would be able to soon. I wanted to make sure I had a good supply ready for my babies.

The fact that I felt like a milk cow was beside the point. I remember when Kianna walked in on me the first time I had the "double pump" hooked up to my breasts. She giggled and asked what I was doing. I have to admit, it did look comical. With visiting the twins, pumping, and seeing family and friends, our days were filled. Visitors barely saw me when they came to the hospital. It seemed like I was always pumping my breasts, and in the presence of others, it would have been uncomfortable for them and for me. My father, however, got used to the whole thing because he and my mother were there so often. He'd respectfully look the other way or try not to acknowledge what I was doing. What a dad.

Since Natania seemed to be holding her own (at least for the time being), the nurses said I could finally hold her. I was excited beyond words. When they handed her to me, she was wrapped in a heavy knit blanket. It was bulky and hard for me to feel her in it. I was concerned that I was not actually holding *her*, and that she might slip right out. I asked if they could put her in a receiving blanket so I could feel her a little more easily.

It was wonderful to hold her and mother her. Something so simple, yet any parent of a preemie or ill baby knows how important it is. She was perfect and so sweet. When she opened her big, round eyes and looked around, it melted my heart. I loved how she hung on tight to my pinkie finger. It felt like a slice of heaven.

Throughout the entire ordeal, when one of us held the girls, we sang to them. We felt it would help them to hear soft, reassuring voices. Awake or asleep, they'd feel content when listening.

Tim was better at singing a variety of songs than I was. His favorite was "Amazing Grace," but he was always interested in learning the lyrics of many "oldies" songs. Unfortunately, mine were a bit more limited. The poor girls heard "Country Road" a lot. Another song I often sang was "You Are My Sunshine." Except I changed it. I could not bear to sing the ending part about taking my sunshine away so I changed it to "I love you more every day." I tried to sing it as written, but I broke down in tears. It was hard to fathom the possibility of losing one of them—I couldn't even go there.

Kianna holds Natania for the first time

CHAPTER 10

I'M READY—THE ROLLER COASTER BEGINS

EVERYTHING UP TO this point seemed good on the surface, but inside I was an emotional wreck. Our family was there to visit, and I tried to remain positive and upbeat about everything. I had no choice since I knew they were all very shaken and were trying hard to hold it together themselves. They were concerned about Tim and me. I could not let them see how frightened I really was. I had to be the strong one, for their sakes.

I knew how difficult it was for my parents to see their little girl going through such a difficult experience. I knew Tim's mother and father were also concerned about us. They always treated me like their own daughter. I did not want them to worry so much. Tim and I also tried to stay positive for each other.

The prayers were overwhelming. The only way I could handle what was going on was to reach out to our friends, church family, and relatives, and ask them to pray for our babies. They were my crutch. The key person, once again, was Jennifer. She was my rock. She was steadfast in her faith, knowing things would be OK.

I remember using the pay phone in the hallway right outside the NICU. Directly dealing with what was happening at that moment was not easy for me, as I found I could not breathe or handle any of it. Instead, I dialed the church and asked them to ask everyone to pray. I felt out of control with everything, and I knew prayer was the only thing I could offer to Natania. I was clutching at anything I could to attempt to help the situation. Quickly I learned what people mean when you hear of someone throwing you a "life-line." This is exactly what happened for me. I was drowning. They threw out the life preserver, and I grabbed on and floated and tried to remember to breathe.

Soon it was Saturday, and my parents and in-laws were visiting the girls with us in the NICU. The mood was serious, yet hopeful, as if there were an unspoken rule that we could not think any other way. The nurses with their warm smiles and reassuring words were fitting. I kept a smile on my face and tried to ignore the severity of what was coming.

I knew I was on the verge of a breakdown. Honestly, I do not know what a breakdown really is. For me, at that moment, I knew I was about to physically collapse. I could not take any of it one second longer. Seeing our tiny baby girls fighting to stay alive was more than I could handle. I forced myself to keep it together while I was with our family. When they were ready to go out, I faked it very well and said that I needed to "talk" to a nurse first and assured them (Tim included) that I would be right there; they could go out.

As soon as I could not see them anymore, my tears erupted. I didn't know where to go or where to turn. I felt sick to my stomach and didn't know what to do with myself. I started searching around the NICU—there was no place for me to go or sit.

Then I saw Lisa (the nurse who spoke to me prior to the girls' birth). I can still see her face in my mind. She was familiar, and she understood. I must have caught her eye. She looked at me with such understanding and started coming toward me, as if she knew she needed to catch me. We walked toward each other at the same time. Then she embraced me and held me as I sobbed uncontrollably on her shoulder. She understood. I was OK with opening up to her and breaking down, something I don't do with just anyone. I let down my wall and allowed myself to be afraid. For a moment, I was no longer strong. She let me be weak and let me know it was OK to be scared.

During this time, the other nurses were so gracious in letting me have my moment as they kept watch over

125

Lisa's tiny patients. They were respectful and seemed for a moment to blend into the woodwork to allow me time to get it out.

I knew Lisa's job was an important one. As soon as I could pull it together, I did. I wanted her to focus her attention on the babies who needed her. I will never forget what Lisa did for me that day. I know I was one of many patients the nurses and doctors help every single day. Saying they "make a difference" is a fraction of the reality of their deep concern and care.

That night, I prayed my heart out again, asking God to prepare me for what was coming. I asked him to let me know the outcome for Natania, and most of all, I prayed for her to be OK. I prayed that she would live to grow, laugh, and play with her sisters and even live to become a mischievous toddler.

From the time the girls were born and we learned of Natania's condition, I was lost. There is no better way to describe it. I was flailing, not knowing what to do or what would happen. I continually prayed for peace. That night, I told God I couldn't handle it and he needed to; I continually prayed for peace.

The next morning was unusual; I actually had my first good night's sleep since the girls were born. When I woke up in the morning, I felt overwhelming peace. I felt ready for whatever was coming. Most of all, it was as if I learned through the power of the Holy Spirit that Natania *was* going to be OK.

No matter what happened, Natania was going to be OK. That was all I needed. I was rested. I was ready. And I was at peace. It was good timing, because that morning, Natania started her downward spiral.

Our roller-coaster life began. Doctors and nurses worked on her quickly. All I remember was hearing them say things like her level of "whatever" was dropping, so they were going to give her this or that. Then they'd tell us something else was dropping, so they'd give her something else.

We were grateful that despite how scary everything was, we knew what to expect, since Dr. Weinhaus prepped us.

We knew that Natania would soon be transported to Children's Hospital in Milwaukee by ambulance. The transport team arrived in their blue jumpsuits, looking like something out of a movie. They moved quickly, with a purpose, like they had done this before. The hardest part of this was learning they needed to change all of the wires/tubes and leads from the hospital's to those of the emergency transport's team. It was extremely hard watching them prep her and get her ready to be transferred. Watching her be poked over and over was so hard to take. No one was happy about it, not even the nurses or doctors. It was the policy of Children's Hospital, so she would be ready when she arrived. That was it. I like to think things are done for a reason, but at that time, all I knew was that they were hurting my tiny baby.

Getting an IV into a baby Natania's size is not an easy feat. Each time they needed to put one in, they needed to surgically place it. This meant they needed to make a small incision into her skin to find the vein. She often had one on her scalp (and they had to shave part of her head for this), as that is usually the best place to find a vein. Once I watched a nurse attempt to get an IV in her, and she was not able to. She called in another nurse, or perhaps it was someone who had special expertise. He could not do it either. As I watched him attempt to insert the IV, his hands shook. They finally said I needed to go out, as they went to "Plan B" (surgically inserting the IV as mentioned before), gently explaining what needed to be done. It was hard to leave our precious baby, knowing what they needed to do to her. I felt I could help if I was simply with her. Maybe I couldn't *help* her, but I could reassure her and let her know she was not alone. I hated it, knowing she was in pain; and I hated knowing what was coming.

As the transport team of NICU specialists continued to prepare Natania, the mood from the St. Mary's staff and the other parents was somber. Mothers watched from the corners of their eyes as they held and rocked their babies. I could tell they felt for us and were worried, but few said anything. I don't think they knew what to say. Some wished us well and told us they'd be thinking of us. The ambulance team was focused, and no one wanted to interrupt what they were trying to accomplish.

Although Natania was breathing on her own, the doctors needed to put a breathing tube in her in case she stopped breathing on the way to the hospital. It was something they preferred not to do in a moving vehicle. It was heart-breaking. They sedated her and proceeded to insert the tube. From that point on, they controlled her breathing. It would be awhile before she would be alert again. We would likely not see her open her eyes until her ordeal was over. I missed her already. She was there, but her personality was temporarily shut down. I continually reminded myself to be strong and to remember the end result.

It was decided that I could not handle the ride in the ambulance, so the plan was for Tim and me to follow the ambulance to Milwaukee. It was difficult, knowing our little baby was inside the ambulance, and not knowing how she was doing.

From this point, it's foggy. Everything happened fast as they settled Natania in their NICU at Children's Hospital. The atmosphere was different from that of St. Mary's. There were a lot more babies, and the mood was busy and clinical. What I remember most was the room they put Natania in. The nurse explained she got the special room because it was where they brought their sickest babies. Wow! Hearing that really affected me!

I remember meeting with Dr. Berger. He was head of the Pediatric cardiology department, and his first priority was to confirm Dr. Weinhaus' diagnosis. Once he did, he came into the waiting room and discussed what was going to be happening. Usually it was difficult to have a discussion like this in a waiting room, since other people might be there. Luckily, we had some privacy.

The doctor told us Natania would need to have her narrowed aorta taken care of immediately. He explained different options, and we all agreed on what was called a "subclavian flap" that could be done safely for a baby her size, without needing to go through her chest. This procedure takes an artery from her shoulder/arm and is used to widen the narrow section of the aorta. They cannot do this with just any patient, as the procedure could result in a child's arm not growing at the same rate as the other arm. Natania's size and prematurity worked in her favor. She was still small enough that her body would "grow" other sources to get the blood to the rest of her arm.

They would enter Natania's body through her side, between her ribs. Going straight through her chest was not safe for a baby her size. As it was, a surgery like this has great risks because of her weight. The surgery itself is fairly common, but it gets trickier the smaller the baby is.

130

The doctor discussed the options to repair the hole in her heart. This could only be repaired through open-heart surgery, which was too risky on a baby as small as Natania. Instead they planned a temporary fix to allow her time to grow before her open-heart surgery. Their plan was to put a "band" on her pulmonary artery to lessen the flow of blood through the hole. The hole caused the oxygenated blood and the non-oxygenated blood to mix together, and the band would keep the blood from backing up into her lungs and buy her time to grow.

Waiting for the surgery was a challenge. At one point, shortly after their birth, I had Tim and my mother find the yellow blanket my deceased grandmother knit for my dolls, the one I used when Kianna was born. I laid it on top of Natania's isolate and felt a sense of comfort, feeling that my grandmother's presence in heaven was with her at all times.

Natania was on the schedule for surgery on Tuesday. Then it was bumped to Wednesday, then Friday. She was on life support, and they continued to maintain her any way they could. Babies with more immediate needs came up, and they needed to take care of them first. The difference was that likely the other babies were not in a position to wait, since they had not been "prepped," as Natania had been. This made their situation more of an emergency.

We discussed our concern about her wait with Dr. Berger. He knew the waiting was killing us, and he also knew we had some concerns about the length of time they were "maintaining" her vs. fixing her.

It was finally confirmed that her surgery would be on Thursday—one week and one day after her birth.

Jennifer and I talked on the phone about the possibility of having her baptized. It was a difficult subject. We didn't want to acknowledge the possibility that we could lose her. It certainly wouldn't hurt, though. After consulting with our pastor, he said it would help us feel more strengthened in our faith, and it would bring Natania more into the faith circle. I do not remember the exact discussion, but Tim and I decided to go along with it.

The details needed to be worked out quickly, so our Pastor in Madison made arrangements with a "sister" church in Milwaukee, whose pastor was the son of church members from Madison. He came and talked to us, and then our little Natania was baptized, right in the NICU, right in the middle of the other babies, parents, and medical staff, separated only by a privacy screen. The nurses got her ready—took her vitals and gave her whatever medications she needed, so they could give us some time.

We were apprehensive about all of it. Baptizing a child in the NICU really puts the seriousness of the situation into perspective, but we tried to remember that she needed all the help she could get. What happened next was just miraculous! Natania opened her eyes for the first time in days and focused on us.

Most babies don't start focusing on things until they are at least a couple weeks old. Here she was, less than three pounds, sedated, and she was actually looking *up* at us and at the pastor, as if she knew it was something important she could not miss. It was wonderful, yet in the back of my mind I prayed it was not her way of saying good-bye. I pushed it out of my mind and told myself it was her way of telling us she was a fighter and would be OK.

The baptism went well. I felt good knowing we went through with it.

That afternoon, the day before her surgery, I was feeling apprehensive and anxious—and sad, weepy, you name it. I was having an "I just want my baby and I want her *now*" kind of feeling. Again, the nurses were great. One of our favorite nurses from Children's Hospital was Mary. She somehow sensed how I felt and asked me if I wanted to hold Natania. Natania had about twenty or more different wires and tubes attached to her, and she was on a ventilator. I didn't believe it was possible.

I asked her if she thought it was OK, and she said, "Yes, I think it is what you both need right now." I was *so* happy to hold my little sweetheart again, but I didn't want to hold her if it meant it could hurt her in any way.

Mary called another nurse to help assist in getting all of the wires and tubes situated so they would not get caught or bent. They took safety pins and pinned them down all around her on her receiving blanket, then gently lifted her up and covered her with another blanket. In order for me to hold her, they took her off the ventilator and manually administered oxygen.

All of this was *so* scary. It felt like absolute *heaven* to hold her in my arms, yet I was afraid something might cause her harm. I wished I could have held her forever and ever, but I also loved her so much that I was willing to forego this wonderful opportunity if it was not good for her. The nurses reassured me.

Shortly after they handed her over, however, her oxygen level dropped. They explained that she needed to have her lungs suctioned out. I'd seen them do this before. They insert a little straw into her ventilator tube and attempt to suck mucus out of her lungs. The tricky part is to insert it into the area where the mucus is built up so they can get it out. I was nervous and asked if we should put her back into her "open bed," but there was not enough time. I had to hold her through it. I didn't want them to have to worry about me freaking out when Natania needed every ounce of their attention. I'd describe myself at that moment as having an out of body experience. I was extremely focused on anything they said and anything I may have needed to do to save my baby. Every precious second was incredibly important.

They proceeded to take turns "bagging" her and suctioning her. When they bagged her, her respiration and oxygen levels would go up. When they suctioned, the levels dropped to a point that made me very nervous. I knew I could not say a word as this went on. I just waited patiently and watched them work together as a team. They were calm and in control. They did not appear nervous, nor did their hands shake. They were all business as they tried to restore her breathing to a healthy level. When they got a good size blob of mucus, they were victorious. With each bit of mucus they removed, her breathing was that much better. Soon they got her back on track. By this point, I had been holding her quite some time, so thankfully I got my fill.

During all of this with Natania, we did not forget about Brialle and Kianna. I don't remember exactly how, but we managed trips back into Madison to see Brialle in the afternoons, then we would see Kianna at my parents (or if they'd met us at the hospital) to have dinner with them and tuck Kianna into bed. We stayed at Ronald McDonald house, walking distance from the hospital in Milwaukee, at a hotel, or at my parents. We made plans minute by minute. As Natania's situation was still grave, Brialle was showing nice improvements. Each time I would say good-bye to one of my girls, I would get tears in my eyes and pray for her safety.

Many of our friends and family were worried about us. We were in survival mode as we were trying to juggle everything. Tim had a wonderful idea to set up a call-in line for people so they could get updates on the girls. We could not call everyone, but this worked out well. He would call each day, record an update, and thank everyone for their prayers. It was intense, but so reassuring, once again, to know so many people were praying for our little angels.

October 27, 1999

I'm finally getting a chance to write. It's been a bumpy road. Natania started showing symptoms Sunday morning . . . I know Natania will be OK. God has let me know. Sunday, when everything was coming to a head, I was finally where I needed to be spiritually. Any earlier, I was not. It's just such a comfort knowing all of the prayers for Natania. The church, our friends, family, and extended family are all praying for our little peanut. We've bonded and gotten to know the girls better. We've still been able to hold Natania, even with the tubes, ventilator, and wires. It was wonderful.

We were finally able to hold Brialle yesterday. She's doing very well. She's off the ventilator and oxygen and is starting tube feedings with my breast milk and is starting to gain weight! It was incredible to hold her. Our little girls

*sure are fighters. They are beautiful! We've been driving
back and forth from Milwaukee to Madison and back to
my parents to see Kianna at night to tuck her into bed. I've
needed to continue pumping, even manually in the car.
It's been interesting. We are headed back to Milwaukee
to see Natania right now. The pastors at the church have
been wonderful. Pastor Sheryl prayed with us before they
were born, then Pastor Kari visited once we heard about
Natania, then Pastor Peter visited yesterday, while we were
in Madison visiting Brialle. God told me Natania will
be OK. I still can't dwell on each fine detail, but I know
the outcome will be very good. When Tim and I saw her
yesterday she tried to open her eyes to look at us, but she'd
sleep again since she is sedated. It's hard to see her like that.
Kianna's doing fine. I miss her too. Soon . . .*

Finally, it was time for Natania's surgery. I assumed
we would be able to meet the surgeon, but as we got
closer to the surgery, we had not. We talked to the
anesthesiologist, the surgeon's assistant, and everyone
else, but not "the guy" himself. I finally asked if I
could meet him. I could tell by the look on the medical
personnels' faces that it seemed like an odd question,
but there was no way I wanted someone to perform such
a risky surgery on my precious baby without meeting

him first. The nurses were understanding and made my request.

At first, the doctor seemed a tad perturbed by my request—I'm guessing he must really need to separate himself from the situation to do what he does every day. As soon as I shook his hand and looked him in the eye, though, he understood. He knew I was a mother who loved her baby. I said to him, "I'm sorry, I know you are very busy, but I needed to meet the man who would be saving our little girl's life. I wanted you to know how much we love her and appreciate what you are doing for us." His eyes softened, and he appeared a bit humbled. He spoke to us for a couple of minutes, and then we were told it was time.

It was the scariest moment of my life. Part of me felt like collapsing, but I just hung on tight to the promise God made me and remembered she would be OK. I feel bad admitting this, but a small part of me was afraid I would never see her alive again. I told God I was sorry for being afraid and that mostly I had complete faith. I got the sense God understood how I felt.

Just before the "crew" started rolling Natania down the hall, after we said our good-byes, Tim said something I will never forget. Thinking about it always makes me feel like crying. He said, "Take good care of her," in a serious, heart-felt, poignant way. They all seemed to stop in their tracks for a moment, and they looked into his eyes. The papa bear had spoken. They got it.

There were no words that seemed appropriate at a time like this, except the words Tim spoke. As a father, he had no control over what was going to happen. He had to put his baby into the hands of strangers and count on them to save her life.

The rest is foggy. The waiting was difficult. Tim didn't want to talk; he was silent and handled what was happening his way. I didn't know what to do with myself. We waited and waited. I think I tried to read some magazines. I think I called Jen.

October 28, 1999

It's 9:54am, and we are waiting to hear how Natania's surgery went. She went in about 8:15am. We thought a nurse was supposed to come out and give us hourly updates. I pray everything is going well. I can't imagine anything but her being OK. God has given us strength and confidence, and everyone has been praying for her. I'm trying to stay calm. It's the longest morning of my life. She was so adorable this morning, her eyes opened as soon as we got here. She's going to be OK. She's our little fighter, our little miracle girl. We love her so, even though she's been at the hospitals and not actually with us, we've been able to connect with her in a very special way.

139

Finally the nurse came out—Martha, the surgeon's nurse. She said the surgery was going very well and that the doctor was pleased. She sat down and talked to us for a couple of minutes while she explained what they still needed to do and when we should be able to see her. We were so relieved. God was watching over her. I could not wait to see her again and just be with her.

5:20 p.m.

The Lord is incredible! She came through the surgery well. The surgeon is apparently a perfectionist, and he was satisfied with how it went. That was because God was guiding him. I am so happy I cannot explain it in words.

She's still sleeping. We are waiting for her to wake up. We are heading back to Mom and Dad's soon, and I hope she does well. Tomorrow we'll give Kianna a ride to school, then see Brialle, then come back here. I miss being with all of my girls! Thank God for today!

The events over the next few days are fuzzy again. Natania was doing well, and she even appeared to be hungry. As her mother, it was as if I knew by instinct that she wanted to eat. She seemed to be doing so well.

The doctors and nurses continued to evaluate her. As her body started taking over, they were able to reduce certain levels of the medications they had been providing for several days. She started to breathe a bit on her own, and when she started breathing "above" the ventilator consistently, they knew she was close to getting off it.

When they took the ventilator tube out, she was fine and breathing on her own. I felt so bad for her though, as her poor little throat was so sore and raw. When she opened her little mouth to cry, nothing came out. We knew she was in pain, but all we could do was reassure her and sing to her.

November 1, 1999

Natania came off her ventilator today! She's on a little oxygen, but it's a major milestone. She was sucking aggressively on her pacifier, like she was starving. They tried feeding her some breast milk over the weekend, but she wasn't quite ready for it. She's been getting nutrients via IV. Today they started 1 ½ cc's of breast milk again. She seems so hungry now. I hope if she tolerates it, they'll increase it regularly. Call it Mom's instinct. Her tummy is ready now. She was awake and very alert today. She was uncomfortable from where her ventilator tube was. I could tell she had a sore throat. Poor peanut. She took some nice yawns, though, to stretch out her little lungs.

Brialle is doing well. She's still a lazy little eater. They suggested I give up on the breast for now to concentrate on the bottle, since she's tired a lot. The nurse commented that she might need a couple of weeks yet before she will be a good "nippler." I try to keep reminding myself that I just need to be patient, and the girls will be home soon enough.

Kianna went trick-or-treating with Daddy last night. She was a very pretty Sleeping Beauty. Kevin and Melissa (dear friends and Brialle's godparents) came over and brought pasties and a gift for Tim's birthday. That was nice. Everyone has been wonderful and helpful. Kianna's been such a big girl with everything. I'm so proud of her.

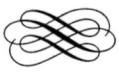

That evening, however, it seemed things were changing. Natania didn't seem to be bouncing back as quickly as she had earlier that day. The nurse continued to evaluate her and reassured us they would get in touch with us right away if there was anything we needed to know. It was horrible leaving her. We had no choice. Visiting hours were over, and we needed to get back to our other girls. There was no major concern from the doctors and nurses, although something in my gut was screaming. We told Natania to be strong and fight and that we would be back first thing in the morning. We left to see Brialle and Kianna that evening, as it had been a couple of days since we had seen them.

When we walked into the NICU the next morning, my legs almost gave out when I saw Natania. I think the blood in my body froze. I thought I was going to get sick. Natania looked like she was moments from dying.

She was white, and her respiration was extremely fast, like she was panting in short breaths. Her heart rate was also very fast. Her left leg looked pasty white, and my instincts told me we were losing her. The nurse, Mary, had taken care of her that entire night. She suspected something was wrong, but she did not know what. She had her back on her ventilator, and she worked around the clock, ordering tests, consulting with various doctors, and getting x-rays to be sure everything was in place for whatever might be happening with her, so they could move quickly.

The nurse looked into our eyes and confirmed that we too felt Natania was struggling. Time was not a luxury for her at that point. I'm not typically one to made demands or seek attention, but as soon as I saw her, I told her we needed to talk to Dr. Berger right away. And she was on it.

Meanwhile, I had to get away from it all. I knew I was essentially handing her over to the doctors. We did all we could do, and we needed to have faith.

Once everything was underway with the doctors, I had to separate myself. I couldn't do anything to help her; I was so powerless. There was only one way to turn—to God. I had to be alone to cry and let it all out. I was afraid for Tim to see me like this. My plan was to pump my milk in a room close by that was specifically set up for this. It was a room with curtains and offered some privacy. This is where I would pray and cry. If someone was there, though, I had to be particularly quiet. That morning, I had the room to myself, and I prayed and cried my heart out, asking God to help Natania. I asked him to help the doctors figure out what was wrong with her and asked him to guide them properly.

When I got out of the room ten minutes later, doctors and nurses and specialists were surrounding Natania. They were all in a heated discussion, trying to figure out what was going on. Dr. Berger, the radiologist, and a hematologist, among others, were "hypothesizing" about her condition. They determined she had a blood clot that was in her descending aorta, around her groin. This was preventing blood from getting to her lower extremity—her left leg. This was also causing major issues with her entire circulatory system.

If they did not do something soon, she would lose her leg, or worse. The medical team was discussing what to do. There is a blood thinning medication they could give her, but they didn't think it would work quickly enough. A surgical attempt to remove it was not an option, as it could make things worse. They finally discussed a very strong medicine that breaks up clots, called TPA. This is what they give adult heart attack and stroke victims, but Natania was less than three pounds, and the risk of brain hemorrhage was great.

The hematologist was clearly concerned about brain damage. The doctors didn't want to have to take her limb or risk her life. Essentially, it was a gamble, as the decision to administer TPA was the lesser of two evils.

In the midst of all of this, Martha gently guided us to the "private room." This is where they take you when you cannot be in the middle of what is happening with your child. It also allows medical staff the opportunity to have a private discussion with the parents. Martha was lovely. She told us what was happening and explained the options. She said she would go back and get an update for us. She came back and explained that the doctors had come up with a good compromise. Rather than administer the TPA through an IV that would circulate throughout her entire body, including her brain, they would re-open the umbilical veins and insert a tiny tube and administer the drug directly above the clot.

None of the doctors had ever tried this on a premature baby before. It was not proven and was a "fly by the seat of the pants" test. But it made sense, and it was something everyone could agree on.

The waiting began again. First, they gave Natania medication that put her body into a coma. This would require the least amount of blood to circulate through her body. For the next couple of days, Natania would be completely lifeless—her body didn't so much as twitch.

As they administered the TPA drug, they watched what was happening on an ultrasound. The side-effect of the medication was that her blood could get so thin that she could have hemorrhaging in her brain, or the clot could break loose and travel to her brain, causing a stroke. Every thirty minutes or so, they monitored her brain activity to watch for "bleeds." I don't recall if it was ultrasound or exactly what equipment they used for this, but each time they checked, we held our breath.

The other issue was the amount of TPA and the length of time it was safe to have the drug in her body. The hematologist and doctors all agreed how long they would continue down this path. Slowly, ever so slowly, the clot started to dissolve. Finally, it was time to take her off the medication. Eventually, we saw the color come back to her face and her leg. It was a miracle, once again. It seemed to have worked. The doctors continued to monitor her brain to watch for bleeds and warned us that she was not out of the woods yet, but things were, so far, going as hoped.

In the middle of this, I remember desperately trying to get to a phone to call Jennifer. I needed to hear her voice, and I needed her guidance. She was my lifeline. As I sat in the NICU, surrounded by all of the babies, doctors, and nurses, she prayed with me and helped strengthen my belief that God would make sure she was OK. We discussed his promise to me. That meant she'd come out of all of this healthy and in one piece (two legs and all)!

Finally, Natania was out of the woods. The doctors seemed encouraged by the way her body responded—all without any problems with her brain, based on everything they could see.

She managed to beat the odds . . . again.

We continued with our travels to Madison, my parent's house, and Milwaukee each day. It sure was lucky to have my parents living half-way between both cities. We got good at managing our new schedule.

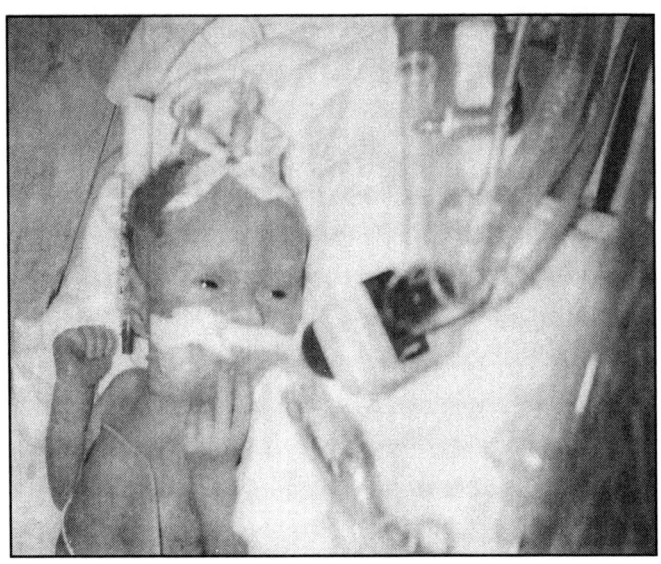

Natania wakes up after her blood clot scare

Manually pumping my breast milk on route to each hospital worked well. If I was headed to Milwaukee, the milk I pumped on the way would be deposited there; if we were headed to Madison, it would go there. It did appear odd to see me doing this in our vehicle. I'd stop whenever we'd see a semi-truck, because I didn't want to expose myself. One time I was not paying attention. I looked up to see a truck driver smiling down at me. It's one thing when you are nursing a baby at your breast; it's quite another when it's a breast-pump machine; but doing it with a manual hand pump was another thing entirely!

Our experience all continued in a blur. It was difficult to continue with our normal life—mail, bills, getting back to people about various things. We were gone almost non-stop once Natania was in Milwaukee. I remember one phone message from Kianna's preschool, Preschool of the Arts. Debbie, a nice lady from the office, called us in the midst of everything to remind us of the Halloween party that was coming up the next day. We quickly rearranged things with my parents to have Kianna attend the parade and party.

Thankfully, back before I was on bed rest with the twins, I had thought to buy her Halloween costume. I knew right where it was and asked my parents to pull it together and take her to the party. The day of the party was the same day as Natania's surgery. It was an emotional day. My father was very emotional watching all of the little children dressed for the Halloween parade having fun while his granddaughter was fighting for her life at the same time. I think his faith was truly tested during this time. He so badly wanted her to be OK. We wanted Kianna to stay busy, and thanks to my parents, she didn't have a lot of time to miss Mommy and Daddy.

We were able to get home once during this time, and what we were going to eat was the last thing on our minds. One day, we arranged for Gail to babysit Kianna while Tim and I visited Brialle at the hospital. Gail also prepared a wonderful meal for us—the best chicken pot pie I ever had—when we got home. When we walked in the door, we heard the fire alarm going off. Gail felt bad because something that had dripped in the oven was burning and caused the alarm to go off. It worked great as an amusing distraction. I tried to get her to understand that it happened to me all of the time because I never get around to cleaning the pizza cheese that drips to the bottom of my oven. The pot pie was just what we needed. Between that and my mother baking some wonderful chocolate chip cookies for us to eat in the car between trips, we were well covered with comfort food. It was surprising that I was able to eat. I was glad I could, because a nursing mother of twins needs nutrition (or maybe I should say a "pumping" mother)!

Natania was finally out of the woods and ready to be transferred back to St. Mary's Hospital in Madison to grow and learn to eat. At the same time, Brialle was ready to be released from the hospital. We were excited to have both of our girls in the same city again.

When Natania was transferred back to St. Mary's, however, her life was once again at risk. I remember pulling into the hospital parking lot. Tim had just been there to see her. When he went to see her in her normal spot, she had been moved to the "other side" of the NICU. The babies were separated, with those on one side requiring normal NICU care and those on the other requiring critical care. Natania had been moved to the critical care side. Tim told me she had a fever and the doctors thought she had contracted a serious bacterial infection. They didn't know yet what bacterial infection she had, but they were already treating it aggressively to be sure they were covering all of the bases. The major concern was that the infection could get into her spinal fluid and eventually her brain. If that happened, she would be gone within hours.

Discovering this is very challenging in preemies. Their bodies do not know how to properly maintain their body temperatures. Thankfully, her temperature rose to 106 degrees to act as a warning to the nurses who caught it.

We waited on pins and needles to learn what kind of bacteria she had in her body and whether the infection had entered her spinal fluid. To determine this, they needed to perform a "spinal tap," where fluid is taken from her spine. A big risk with very small babies during a spinal tap is that they can hit the spinal cord when taking the fluid—this would cause instant paralysis.

The spinal tap went well, but when we finally learned the results, we were shocked to hear she had contracted E. coli. The doctors and nurses could not figure it out. They said the body naturally has this bacterium in the bowels and digestive tract, but it somehow got into her bloodstream. After giving it a lot of thought, I suspected she may have gotten it through the continuous pokes she received in her heels, as they were always checking her blood counts/levels. During a diaper change, babies scrunch their legs up, and their heels can easily get into the mess, thus getting it into their bloodstream.

Natania was fortunate once again—she beat the odds. Because of the nurse's quick determination that there was a problem, they were able to treat her condition before it was too late. Amazing!

Finally, Natania was on the road to recovery. Really. She slowly but surely started to gain weight. She learned how to suck from a bottle, and she was getting stronger. There were many times when she would gain one ounce one day, then lose one the next. It often seemed like one step forward, two steps back. We would celebrate each ounce and become discouraged when she lost weight. This is a familiar cycle for parents of a preemie. And it is normal. But at the time, the worry is so great, and parents wonder if things will ever start heading in the right direction.

November 22, 1999

We'll see how much I can write before little Brialle wakes up. Yes, she's home. Two weeks today. It's wonderful. Natania is still in the hospital. She might have been home within a week, but she developed an infection. It is clearing up, but she's going to need to stay on antibiotics for a long time to make sure it does not settle into her heart area.

The day after I wrote last, Natania started showing symptoms of a blood clot. She almost lost her leg. It was terrifying. We got to the hospital in Milwaukee, and she looked terrible. I just about fainted when I saw her that morning. She was very pale/gray, and she was breathing so fast. I thought she was dying.

With God's help, the doctors were guided to find the problem quickly.

CHAPTER 11

TWIN ADVENTURES

AFTER THE TWINS were out of danger with their health, Brialle was able to come home. The timing worked nicely for Natania to be transferred back to Madison to heal and grow. Caring for a four-year-old and a newborn was a challenge, although doable. Fitting in trips to the hospital with a newborn on a heart rate/ respiratory monitor was harder than I imagined. Mostly I was upset that Natania was not at home where she belonged. It broke my heart each time I had to say good-bye to her. It made me feel better knowing Tim also went to see her twice each day—early in the morning before the doctors did their rounds (parents were not allowed during rounds back then), as well as after work early in the evening.

Our nights were packed with the excitement of not only having a newborn at home but also with the monitor. The monitor had wires that attached to her chest, back, and stomach, and detected her heart beating and her breathing. If either stopped, a loud, piercing alarm would immediately sound. The lead wires attached to Brialle often got loose or fell off, sounding the alarm, and of course, it always seemed to happen in the middle of the night. I would have loved to have had a video camera to capture Tim and me literally leaping out of bed at the same time, practically fighting to get to her first. I usually knew to give in and let him win, since he is bigger than I am, and I was still recuperating from the C-section. While we knew chances were she was fine and it was likely another loose lead, we always worried—what if?

Before we could take her home, we were required to take infant CPR classes, but when really faced with an emergency, you hope you remember what to do. When dealing with small babies, helping them to breathe again is a delicate challenge. Thank God it was a challenge we did not need to face.

To visit Natania, I hauled a big double-stroller and Brialle's monitor into the back of our Suburban every day. In addition to this, I had to get Brialle and Kianna ready to go. Typically, just when I thought I was ready, Brialle would need another feeding, or she would suddenly need a diaper change (a.k.a. "blow out"). This resulted in the need for a quick bath and a change of clothes. I don't think I was ever on time getting anywhere.

When we finally got out the door, our first stop was Kianna's preschool. We decided to continue with Kianna in preschool since we felt it would be best to keep her routine. I was not allowed to expose Brialle to a preschool environment yet, so I was grateful that the teachers allowed me to park illegally so I could walk Kianna quickly to the door. Then her teacher took her to her classroom. At pick-up time, I'd do the same thing. The teacher would walk her out to me so I didn't have to leave Brialle unattended in the car.

Once Brialle and I got to the hospital, I'd put her in the back part of the double stroller; it was the kind you could snap the infant car seat right in. Her monitor was in the front seat of the stroller since it needed to be attached to her. It worked out well, with one exception—my clumsiness in trying to steer the big stroller, particularly through the NICU. I had to be careful to dodge the many monitors and the equipment throughout the department.

My heart would be full yet sad when I'd see our little Natania. She spent each night alone. Although the nurses were the greatest, it was not the same. Seeing her was so wonderful. Usually Brialle napped in the stroller, so I could pick up Natania. I was excited when she was strong enough to take a bottle instead of the feeding tube through her nose. They used cute little bottles made just for preemies. It took her awhile, but she eventually got the hang of it. They still had a good supply of my breast milk for her, but it would go fast. I was struggling with how to fit in pumping my milk, nursing Brialle full time, caring for Kianna, and visiting the hospital. Sometimes my mother accompanied Brialle and me to the hospital. Having an extra set of hands when Brialle needed attention was heaven.

The trips to the hospital each day continued. At Thanksgiving, Natania was still in the hospital. It was difficult that she was not with us, but we visited her in the morning, and again after we celebrated Thanksgiving at our home with my parents and brother. My father had printed out a bunch of "Turkey" stickers from his computer to give to Kianna so she could hand them out to the medical staff at the hospital. Natania was doing well, and it was only a matter of time before she could come home.

Spending a holiday at the hospital is hard to explain. We knew the nurses and doctors were also balancing their time at the hospital away from their families. They were kind and understanding when we all came to see Natania on Thanksgiving. Dad and Kianna brought enough "Turkey" stickers for the entire staff. I think they stuck them to their nametags or the backs of their hands to share in the holiday spirit.

Unfortunately, around this time we learned that things were not always going so well for other babies. After one evening visit, Tim came home feeling bad after witnessing another family having to say good-bye to their baby. While our twins were finally on the right track, another family was grieving. He saw a family sobbing as they held their deceased baby in their arms for the last time. We also learned of another family who had twins with a similar history as ours—differences in size, etc.—and they lost one of the twins. It was difficult to hear. Why them? We almost felt guilty, and our hearts went out to the other families.

Everyone in the NICU had a common bond, and we all understood each other. Seeing one of us go through such pain was unbearable. There were so many families experiencing so many different challenges.

For those of you who have gone through a significant loss of a loved one, it can be hard to understand why some live while others die. It doesn't seem fair. Only God understands the greater picture and purpose in life. I never attempt to know all of the answers, but I know that some day I will learn them when I am in heaven myself.

On a lighter note, I will never forget the first time I was at the hospital *alone* and Natania was finally able to come with me and Brialle to the "family room" adjacent to the NICU. I was excited to get the girls together again. My hope was for them to be awake and "bond" a bit. They were so adorable, but most of the time one of them slept while the other flailed around, giving her sister a punch in the mouth. Then one decided she was hungry, so I made sure the other was safe on the couch (they were too little to worry about rolling yet), and I proceeded to feed her. Then the other cried to be fed.

Hmmmm, I thought. *Now what?* The nurses were not around, and I was alone. How would I manage this? I laughed to myself. I knew this was a moment I'd never forget. I also knew what I was in for in the coming months (and years). Natania was not strong enough to nurse well yet, but we were working on it. It took a lot of patience and time to help her understand what nursing was all about. I was grateful that Lisa came in to help. She was confident and matter-of-fact, and she helped with Brialle, while simultaneously helping me coax Natania to nurse.

The time finally came for Natania to be released from the hospital. We were so excited. My biggest dream was to have all of my girls and Tim snuggling together in our bed, and for me to hold all of my girls in my arms. I couldn't wait until they were all safe under one roof and together.

I wanted my dream to be complete and fulfilled, as if we were going to go back to make things the way they should have been in the first place—bringing our girls home, together. My parents offered to stay at our house with Kianna (and Otis, our dog) to wait for our arrival. We were beaming as we walked in the hospital, pushing the stroller with Brialle and knowing the additional infant car seat would soon be filled too. My mother knitted two beautiful (tiny), yellow sweaters with hoods for the girls.

The hospital staff treats a preemie who is going home as a celebration. They take pictures of their "graduate." In our case, they took one of the girls together in their matching sweaters and matching purple fleece carrier covers to keep them warm. Although Natania was just four pounds, she was on her way home with her family.

We were a bit nervous now that we were completely responsible for the girls. Yet at the same time, it felt

Bringing home *both* babies

159

exhilarating to know that we could finally be the parents of all of our girls. In the hospital, the nurses taught us that the girls wouldn't break, and they helped us realize we were capable and confident. They taught us how to feed them through the feeding tube, change them, take their temperature, dress them, and even encouraged us when we hesitated. The doctors and nurses at St. Mary's Hospital were so helpful to us. Although they take care of so many babies and their parents day after day, they made us feel special and treated us like they really cared about our children and us.

December 25, 1999

It's Christmas and we have a lot to celebrate! We have two babies at home. Natania came home December 8! She's doing great. I have not had time to write, as can be imagined. We've had little sleep, so every chance I get I try to nap (more like clean). Last Tuesday the girls were (weighed)—5.1 and 8.3! Brialle has been quite the eater.

December 26, 1999

I could not finish yesterday. My opportunities to write will be few and far between. Anyway, I love being a mom. Despite the fact that I'm tired more than before, it's really great. It's been more hectic now with the holidays, but I'm looking forward to every day. The hardest part is when they want to eat at the same time. . . . Looking back (at what we've been through) I wonder how we really did get through. We had no choice but to take it one step at a time. God shielded me from too much pain. I think back to when Natania was on the "open bed" waiting to be transported to Milwaukee and all the many, many tubes she had. The other mothers looked at me with pity in their eyes. I've been in both shoes. Except this time it was my child. God walked with us . . .

CHAPTER 12

SLEEP DEPRIVATION AND CREATIVE JUGGLING

M Y JOURNAL ENTRIES were few and far between after the twins were born. Life got pretty chaotic, being parents of twins, a little girl, and a dog. I was fortunate enough to stop working when the twins were born. The timing worked out nicely; about the same time, Tim got a promotion. The promotion meant his responsibilities were greater, but it also helped balance my loss of income.

While we both made the decision for me to stay home with the girls, and although I was very grateful to be able to, it was difficult for me to be financially dependent on Tim. I felt bad that I was struggling with my new role. I loved my girls, yet I never felt like I was succeeding in the demands of being a stay-at-home mom. Looking back, it had much to do with sleep deprivation.

If you're familiar with "Maslow's Hierarchy of Needs," you know sleep is one of your most important and basic needs. I was typically known as being an upbeat, positive person, but without sleep, I sometimes turned into a crabby zombie. Sometimes I was so exhausted, I just wanted to collapse. Often I would start to cry, and just ensuring my babies' safety was all the energy I could muster. My short-term memory was not very good, and I felt like I was always in a daze. I'd joke with my friends that they never really knew me being 100%. First I was on an emotional roller coaster with the hormonal medications and fertility treatments for so long. Then I was pregnant and out of it, and now I was desperately sleep deprived. Some day, when things calm down and my kids are older, I might come around again.

When the twins were nursing, I tried not to wake Tim during the nighttime feedings. It was difficult at the time. I could not nurse both of them at the same time. I remember the second I heard one of them, my plan was to bolt out of bed and pick up the one baby and feed her before she woke her sister, then wake up the other for her feeding. I tried it several different ways, but this was the best. If I just fed the one and went back to sleep, it never failed—the other would be up about ten minutes after I fell back to sleep. As it was, this went on every hour and a half. Natania took about twenty-five minutes to nurse—as I tried to keep her awake to get a good feeding—and Brialle took about twenty minutes.

When you consider the next round started an hour and a half later, it meant a whopping forty-five minutes of sleep, forty-five minutes to feed, all night long. Yep, sleep deprivation was brutal. Very brutal.

Sometimes, of course, they both woke up at the same time, wanting to be fed. Still not asking for help, I attempted to nurse them at the same time. I could not sit in the rocking chair, because both would have their bodies to each side of me, and there was not enough room. So I had to sit on the floor. We had a "Boppy" pillow, but as I attempted to get one to feed, the other would lie on the floor, screaming her little head off (well, practically). Then, just as the one would "latch" on, I'd try to get the other baby on, and wouldn't you know, the other would fall off again. I tried everything, from getting more pillows around me to help prop them, to trying to lift both at the same time and let them figure out how to latch on themselves.

It was comical, but when you are exhausted and both of the babies are screaming at the top of their sweet little lungs, it didn't seem so at the time. We were exasperated at the situation. One time, Tim came stumbling in with the funniest look on his face as he was rubbing his eyes. "Do ya need some help?" As hard as I tried to go it alone, I really needed his help. He attempted to help me get both latched on, and once they were nursing happily, I sent him back off to bed. He had to be 100% the next day at work and couldn't take a nap during the day, so we agreed I'd go it alone as much as possible. I felt bad waking him up, but that is just part of having children, particularly twins. I'd try to catch up on my rest on the weekends.

Kianna was a trooper with her sisters. She had always been a strong little girl. She had to be so independent, but she never complained. She tried to help whenever possible; she even changed diapers. Once when I was nursing one of the babies, she tried to help by changing the diaper of the other. I videotaped her while I was nursing one baby, and it was funny to watch as Kianna tried to change her wiggly sister while she screamed her head off.

We loved taking the girls for walks. Often, when my parents came to help out—which was a *lot*, we would get the girls in their double strollers and their matching outfits and bonnets and get them into the fresh air. Usually Kianna would be bouncing and jumping all over the place, telling us all about preschool, her dreams, or anything else she could think of. Or she'd ask to help push her baby sisters. She was (and still is) the proudest big sister there is, and she is incredibly protective of them as well.

When I was a little girl, I loved pushing babies in strollers. A good friend of our family, Helen, told me about the many times she'd take her babies out for a stroller ride, and I was right there, asking to push. Her babies have kids of their own now (one is Tania I mentioned after our Maui trip who has twins), but I must have been around Kianna's age at the time and loved being around them. I also always loved dolls. For some reason though, I never had a stroller for my doll. Once I tied a string to a box and dragged it around with my doll in it. I couldn't wait until the day I had my own baby to push in a real stroller.

One thing about having twins (particularly identical) is people stop you all the time. I do the same thing. I have several friends who have twins. We have had times when people stop us in the mall or other public places and ask a lot of questions or ask if they are twins. This is usually fine, and as a proud mother I am happy to answer their questions. The problem comes when one or both of the babies are screaming or when you know you are getting close to feeding time (maybe your body is telling you that too; nursing moms know what I'm talking about here), and you are rushing to get home so you can feed them.

There were times I'd attempt to feed them when we could find a decent place so I could nurse them, but often that is a challenge in public. At times, I would have a bottle for one and nurse the other at the same time. How, you wonder? One would be in the stroller, and I'd use one hand to give the bottle after I'd get the other baby latched on my breast. Yes, even though I'd be in a more "private" place, maybe in the sitting area of a rest room, I'd get a lot of attention or comments that I had my hands full. When Kianna was not at preschool, she would come with me and help me feed a baby. Always the helper!

Natania continued to be smaller than Brialle. Although they looked alike, Natania sadly looked liked a smaller version of Brialle. People always asked, "Are they twins?" When I said yes, they'd always follow with, "But this one is smaller than the other," as if to challenge me. Yes, people say the darndest things. I didn't like to get into a big discussion on why, so I'd shut them up with a quick statement, "Yes, the smaller one had a rough start; we are just happy she is with us." I was not trying to make them feel bad, but sometimes people need to think before they speak.

CHAPTER 13

HERE WE GO AGAIN

ONCE THE GIRLS were home and we were getting used to our new life, one of the regularly scheduled doctor appointments indicated Natania's body was beginning to show signs of needing her open-heart surgery. The hope was for her to hit nine pounds before she had surgery to repair the large hole in her heart. We needed to prepare ourselves for what was going to happen.

February 28, 2000

Natania needs her surgery. It is scheduled for March 2. I'm such a mix of emotions. Most of me knows everything will be OK, part of me is scared, and part of me just wants to crumble. I love her and all of my girls so much. I'm afraid of losing her, but I know God is with her. He has plans for her, and my worry is not of God. God forgive me and give me peace that she'll be OK. I'll write more soon. I can't wait until this is a distant memory.

We planned to have my parents take care of Kianna and Brialle so we could focus on Natania. Natania's surgery was again at Children's Hospital in Milwaukee. We stayed at my parents the night before her surgery so we could head out early the next morning. We left a note for the girls and told them to say prayers for their sister and that we would talk to them soon.

While we could feed Natania up until midnight, trying to explain to a four-month-old why she cannot eat the morning of her surgery was not happening. She was upset off and on because she was so hungry. We were allowed to offer a bit of Pedialite, but she wanted nothing to do with it. Although she was hungry, managing just one baby (and having my husband there) was so simple.

When it came time for her to be admitted, she was the sweetest baby. She was smiling and enjoying the attention of two parents and all of the nurses. We were nervous, of course, but trying to stay calm and happy so she would not pick up on anything. The nurses had us change her into a baby medical gown. It had little frogs on it. We made a big fuss about her outfit, and she "ate it up." Tim had her laughing and smiling as we waited.

After some additional testing and questions, it was time. I remember we were in some type of "holding area" for a while, and we talked to the anesthesiologist and other nurses. I will never forget when they told me it was time for us to hand her off. They carry the babies into the surgical room, since being rolled off on the bed away from the parents might alarm them. I believe they may have given her something orally for her to become sleepy ahead of time, and they waited until it took effect before they administered the IV.

They carried her off, and that was it. I watched as my sweet little girl was being walked away in the arms of a young, male nurse through the swinging surgery doors, until I could not see her anymore. I felt helpless and afraid. It's hard to put into words. I remember turning away as I felt tears build up in my throat, and I gasped for air. Tears spilled out of my eyes. I felt so helpless and out of control. I prayed quietly and pleaded with God to be there watching over her and guiding the doctor's hands.

My baby's body would soon be cooled to a very low temperature while they entered through her rib cage. She would be put on a heart and lung by-pass machine, which essentially pumps the blood and oxygen outside of her body so they can work on an empty heart. During this time, her heart was outside of her body as well. Her little heart was only about the size of a walnut. The heart surgeon needed to open up her heart and sew a patch about the size of a pencil eraser over the hole. Most of the details are limited because it was too much for me to take in. I didn't want to know everything they were doing to my baby. I just blocked it out and focused on the end result . . . and continued to pray my heart out.

March 2, 2000

12:25 p.m.

Natania is still in surgery. We are waiting to hear if they will close her up. So far the nurse says it is going fine. They closed the hole and are beginning to warm her heart back up. It's just amazing what they can do. Thank God for the doctor and his staff! Praise God! It's been tough. It's so hard imagining how/what they are doing to her. She's my baby, and I'm sitting here while she's fighting for her life—without me. She was so sweet this morning, smiling and calm. It's hard to put into words how we feel. I just thank God for watching over her. The nurse is supposed to give another update at 1 p.m. I pray they are thrilled with their work.

After what seemed like a very long time, the nurse came out. I searched her face for a hint of how things were going. She had a lovely, calm smile on her face. *That is a good sign*, I thought. She told us the surgery went perfectly. I loved that word. I was so grateful. She said the doctor was able to get in and position the mesh patch in her heart and that it all went very well. In fact, she said the doctor himself was pleased. I felt warm and happy, and I thanked God over and over. It was as if he was holding her and us at the same time as we went through this.

When we saw Natania for the first time after her surgery, she was puffy and sleeping. I wanted to pick her up in my arms and never let her go. She actually looked more like Brialle. She came out of her anesthesia well and was on the road to recovery. Meanwhile, my parents and Tim's parents were helping with Brialle and Kianna. Since Natania was older now, we didn't want her to be alone, so Tim stayed by Natania's side for three straight days and nights while she was in intensive care. I stayed with Brialle and my parents and Kianna at the Ronald McDonald house. The Ronald McDonald house helps families who have enough to worry about, and the house is warm and inviting. It was perfect. They even found a room that had a small separate room for Brialle—furnished with a crib. Since I was nursing Brialle, I couldn't be away from her for long, so this arrangement was perfect.

The day after Natania's surgery, the grandparents, Brialle, and Kianna came to see her. We knew Brialle was likely a bit confused, wondering where her little friend went. It was so precious when they saw each other again. We lifted Brialle up so she could see her sister. Their little faces lit up. I was so grateful they were able to see each other.

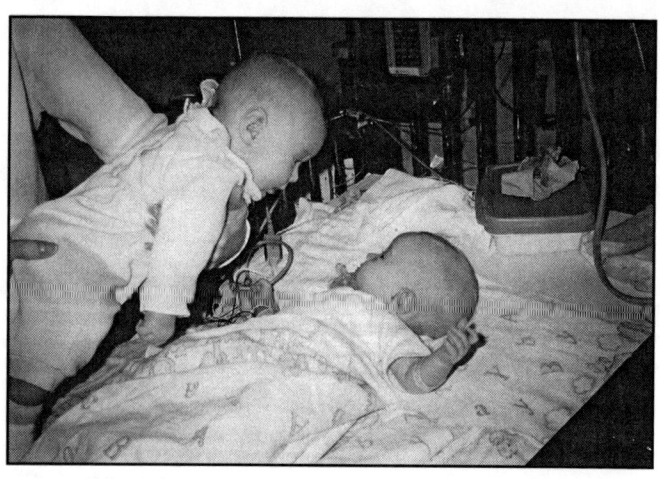

**Brialle wonders, "Where have you been?"
when seeing Natania after surgery.**

When Natania was transferred out of the NICU into her own room, the staff brought in a cot for me to sleep with her, and I could bring in the "Pack and Play" for Brialle. I was so happy I could be with both girls.

When Natania was sleeping, she seemed very agitated. I am allergic to morphine. It makes me jumpy, and I cannot sleep well without jerking myself awake. It was an awful feeling. I suspected perhaps this was happening with Natania too. They gave her a pacifier to calm her, but whenever it fell out of her mouth, she cried. She really depended on it. Needless to say, I didn't get a lot of sleep. It was about every fifteen minutes or so that the pacifier fell from her mouth. I also had Brialle there, and she typically woke up two or three times each night to nurse. Since the girls were born early and small, their feedings were more frequent than full-term babies.

During her stay, I was upset by a major oversight by a nurse. She obviously did not take the time to read Natania's chart and learn why she was in the hospital. The nurse proceeded to lift Natania up under her arms. "She just had open-heart surgery," I said, alarmed. "You can't pick her up like that!" A baby cannot talk, but I could. Thank God I was there! I could only imagine the pain Natania felt. We were taught how to lift her under her head and torso so we would not hurt her chest. I was very angry. I'm not the type to come down on people, but I talked to the physician's assistant and told her that there was no excuse for that and that they needed

175

to make sure it never happened again. The PA was very nice. She took my comments and suggestions to heart.

At another point in the night, one of the nurses came in while Brialle was stirring. Most moms know that during the night, you try hard not to stimulate the baby; communication is minimal and down to business. Well, she took one peek at Brialle and said, "Oh, hello, sweetie!" Oh boy, I knew I was up for the rest of the night at that point. Brialle was full of it and eating up all the attention. Then the nurse left, and Brialle cried to be fed. Then Natania cried again. Hmm. Brought back memories. Although this time I wanted to avoid Natania crying at all costs, because I knew crying could hurt her.

I knew this was a unique situation, although I realized if I had not been there, a nurse would have taken care of her—so I swallowed hard and called the nurse for help. I didn't know what else I could do. If I stopped nursing Brialle, then she would continue to cry and wake up Natania, and it would become a vicious cycle. We got through it though. As with anything, I had to remember: this too will pass.

At one point, toward the end of Natania's stay, we were allowed to escort her out of her room to the cafeteria. We had our first family meal since her surgery. Although Natania was still hooked up to her IV's and other paraphernalia, we proudly marched her down with our friends Kevin and Melissa. While we were eating,

Tim introduced Brialle to French fries and was teasing me for being over protective about what we were feeding her. We were so relaxed and grateful that Natania's ordeal was over.

It was amazing, but Natania was home in only one week. She was happy and smiling, and you'd never know she'd just gone through open-heart surgery.

March 8, 2000

We are on our way home! Natania's surgery went well, without complications! Praise God! We are in our Suburban, and the girls are all packed up and just fell asleep in their car seats. Natania should be tired, she was up from 1:30am–5:30am last night, or I should say this morning! She loves her new heart! I'm going to take a nap now.

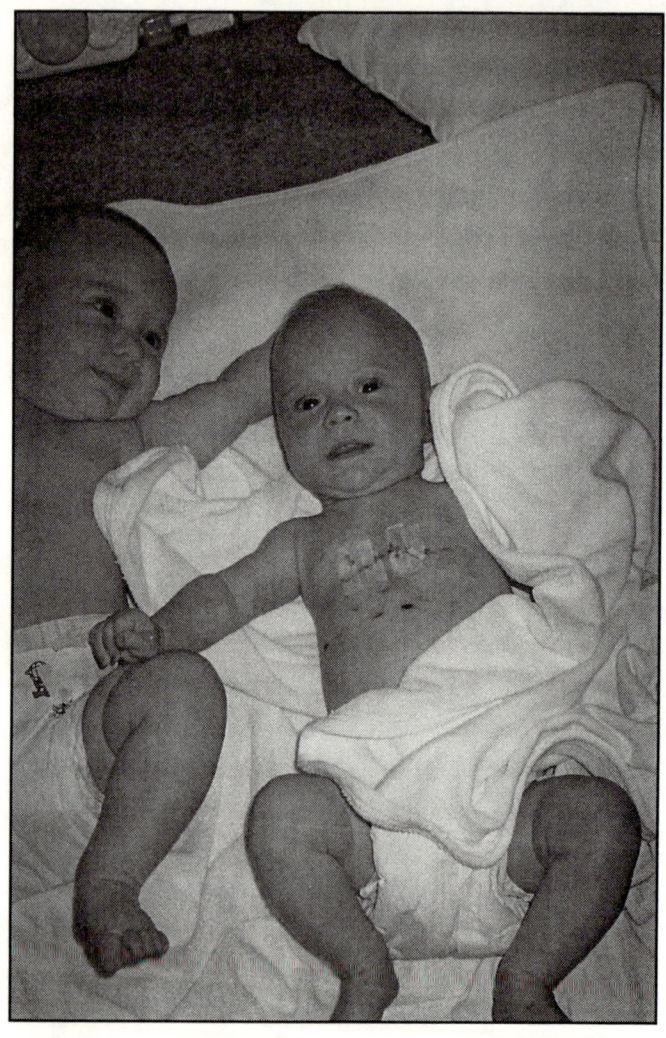

Natania recovering well at home after second surgery.

CHAPTER 14

EVERY OUNCE
MATTERS

I WANTED TO THINK everything would be fine after Natania's heart was fixed up. It was not realistic, I suppose. It is easy to have an idealistic view on how things should go. She had heart defects, and then they are fixed, and now we move on, right? Not so simple. After her second heart surgery, she never really thrived. This means she did not gain appropriate weight.

We spent a lot of time with specialists, trying to figure out why. Our quest for answers were sought with many tests, from Cystic Fibrosis to Celiac disease and bone-growth testing, as well as many blood tests that ruled out other problems such as leukemia, to barium tests to look at her digestive tract.

Natania was not taking in enough calories to gain the weight she needed. Anything she took in was burned off in living. We even met with a specialist to help Natania with her eating aversions.

One thing we were able to determine was that Natania had some damage to her phrenic nerve that led to her diaphragm. One half of her diaphragm was not working properly, therefore, causing her to breathe rapidly. The doctors said it was hard for her to drink from a bottle because she had to work so hard to breathe. She was also at an increased risk for pneumonia, because it was difficult for her to take big, deep breaths.

It was a full-time job just making sure I was giving her any medications needed and always focusing my energy on how many calories she was taking in. We met with a dietician to figure out ways to sneak a few extra calories into her each day. While other people are looking at the nutritional value/calories and fat on their food labels because they are trying to reduce their calorie intake, it was the opposite with us. I learned that Maria's Macaroni and Cheese, for example, was packed full of fat and calories, and I'd load up on that. I tried to cook meals, adding additional calories whenever possible. I offered Natania the high-calorie foods first, so she didn't fill up with the fruits and veggies and be too full for the "good stuff."

My mother got to the point where she could tell if Natania had a good day with her eating by the tone of my voice when I answered the telephone. On bad days, I wished I could open up her mouth and stuff her with food so she'd grow and be healthy. "The harder you try, the worse it gets" is what the doctors told us, so I had to try hard not to make a big deal out of it.

With all of her health issues, and her size, she also had a compromised immune system, so we had to be careful of germs. We still have not taken them to the typical "kid-play restaurants." Getting together with friends and family was stressful. If another child came to our home with a cold, it could potentially send Natania to the hospital. A cold itself is one thing, but children with a compromised immune system can have complications, such as pneumonia.

It was difficult to explain to friends and family why we could not attend events or socialize as much as most people do. We didn't want to offend anyone, but some people couldn't understand why my mother, for example, could come and spend time with us and hold the babies, but they couldn't. The more people we exposed them to, the greater the risk. I remember a time when a friend popped in with her kids in tow, wanting to visit. I was so preoccupied watching which toys went into her baby's mouth that I don't think I heard a word she said. As soon as she left, I grabbed the toys and sanitized them.

Some people would make light of our situation, probably attempting to make me feel better with their so-called helpful comments by minimizing my concern. As Natania's mom, I knew what was going on, from when she was on the verge of pneumonia just by listening to her breathing, to knowing if she needed to be nebulized or be taken to the ER, to being in tune with her if she was coming down with a new bug. Her pediatrician always took my concerns seriously and knew my judgment was good when it came to my girls.

When Natania was at the height of her eating aversions, it became too difficult to rely on my parents so much for help. I've always been afraid to ask for help, but I finally called the church to ask if they had any people available who might be able to help. Natania was to the point where she wouldn't eat if someone else was around—including her twin sister. When I was alone, I would try to feed Brialle first and then put her in her crib upstairs, sometimes crying, so I could feed Natania. Tim and I invested in a video monitor system so I could at least keep an eye on Brialle when she was fussing so I knew she was safe.

We learned of a woman named Esther, who lived nearby. She was willing to volunteer some help, but I couldn't stand the thought of Esther helping us for free when there were so many other people/moms out there who needed help. I insisted on paying her. Although she continued to reject my attempts, we finally agreed that the money could be a donation back to the church. I told her otherwise I would not feel right about accepting her help. It was nice when she was there. She could feed Brialle (or hold Natania when I fed Brialle) in a different room while I fed Natania. Brialle was tickled to have the extra attention. We called her "Grandma Esther," and although she was not an official grandmother yet, she would soon be busy helping her own grandchildren.

We later hired another person to help out as well, particularly when Esther was not available. Her name was Danielle. She was a young woman with a big heart. She loved children, and the girls loved her. She was capable and helpful. Her smile could light up a room.

Many of our friends offered assistance in various ways. The wife of Tim's coworker, Julie, pitched in when the girls were first home by giving Kianna rides to preschool a couple of times each week. It helped tremendously. It was a great time saver, not having to bundle up the girls and try to get Kianna to school on time.

Kianna also continued to do her part. When the girls were starting rice cereal, Kianna loved to help feed them. I laugh when I think of some video we have when she was trying to multi-task—watching TV while feeding her sisters. Her attention would be split, and she'd have the spoon with the cereal on it, and just as she would *almost* get it to them, she'd look at the TV. The girls would try to follow their mouths to the spoon. It would instead almost go into their ear or maybe even their nose. At least she meant well, right? It was funny to watch, that is for sure.

Thinking back on the wonderful generosity we received from people like Esther, Danielle, and other friends, I'm touched at how God brought people into our lives at just the right time. I hope He puts me in a situation to do something to give back someday when I have the opportunity.

April 2, 2000

Things are going well. Brialle is just like any 5 ½ month old, and it is such a blessing to see her so healthy. Natania has a small area of her lung that has collapsed. She also has slowed down with her growth. She's on a nebulizer as of today. I pray to God it breaks up the mucus so her lungs open up. I also pray she really starts growing. It's like she's happy getting by on less. She eats OK, but not like Brialle. She wants the breast only (prefers) and then wants peace and quiet. Otherwise she gets mad or too interested in what is going on around her to eat. But she giggles like no one else. She's so funny and has such a wonderful smile, as do Brialle and Kianna.

Brialle squeals and tries to get you to play. Everything goes into her mouth. She hangs on tight when you feed her—to your hand if with bottle, or to my clothes if I nurse her.

Kianna has been doing well. She's such a doll. . . she is such a great help with the girls. She sings to them and plays with them. Brialle calls out to her if she walks away. Natania watches everything she does. Natania loves to watch me comb/brush Kianna's hair. She's a hair person. It's funny. Brialle stands well. Natania is 10 lbs. Brialle is about 14.

A Few days later . . .

I worry about our little Natania. They are treating her for pneumonia, so now she's on an antibiotic too. We have to give Lasix 2 times a day, nebulize 3 times a day, and now give Augmentin 2 times a day, as well as her vitamins. That's a lot to keep track of. She hates the medicine.

She only gained 1 oz. since last week. Then I fed her and she gained 4 oz. Plus she had a BM right before we left (for the doctor). I pray she'll start eating better and get over all of this.

I just feel like crying for a long time. I feel sick about it. It's hard. I try to stay strong, thanks to God, but sometimes I just want to cry. I love our children so much. I want them to be healthy. The hardest thing I've ever had to do is see my children in pain and trust in God alone. The trusting God part is good and easy, yet it does mean letting go. Instincts make that difficult, but I need to remember that they are God's children first! That is easier said than done. But it is true. God wants what is best!

Please, God, help Natania to be healthy and show signs of improvement every day, and thank you for all the rest of us and our good health. I'm becoming so attached to the twins and they to me. It's addicting. They are. I love Kianna so much and never thought I could love more children as much as I love her, but I do. I miss them when I'm away for a couple of hours. Please, God, help Natania. Amen.

May 2000

I've been handling so much for so long that I'm shutting down. I'm sick with worry over Natania. She only breastfeeds and usually only gets the front milk so she doesn't get the calories. Her diaphragm is apparently the problem (the nerve to her diaphragm was damaged during surgery). It's why she breathes so fast—one side isn't functioning properly. She burns up so many calories just breathing.

May 21, 2000

I'm better now. Natania is up to 11 lbs. as of last Friday. They've been very concerned about her weight gain. Friday to the previous Friday, she finally gained 5 oz. in 7 days. But the two weeks prior only 4 oz in 2 weeks! She won't eat solids either. They were getting concerned about that, but I reminded them she was 7 weeks early and is now like a 5 month old. I pray she starts eating solids. God, please help. Brialle is 15.4 lbs. She's doing wonderfully. Kianna is my big girl. So hard to believe she's 4, going on 5. I love my girls so.

It's difficult to drag the twins to the doctor each week, sometimes more. I'm having a hard time accepting the condition the house is in. I can't wait to get it all clean when Mom and Dad come. They are coming on Tuesday this week. I realize I never consistently cleaned every day, although when I had energy, you couldn't stop me. Now I might have the energy but can't.

May 25, 2000

Jen's in town. It's so great to see her; she's such an incredible person. Her dad is in the hospital. He had a lot of complications, but thank God he is better now. He was transferred out of ICU today. I saw her yesterday. First she stopped out at the house, then I met her at the hospital for lunch. We had a wonderful time. We have not had the opportunity to talk like that in forever.

June 9, 2000

Natania and Brialle are weaned. I needed to wean because Natania just wasn't growing well. Although she had been sick and not doing as well with eating, I felt the breast milk was not cutting it anymore. I started my cycle, and I think that it changes the quality and taste of the milk.

August 3, 2000

It's been hard to find time! Everyone is doing well, although Natania is still very small and not growing and not wanting to eat well yet. They are such a blessing. Tim's been great too. It's always a struggle to feed Natania. She still won't eat baby food. She's 12 ½ lbs. Brialle is 17 lbs. Natania's personality does not help. She gets so excited about her surroundings and is so active that she'd rather do anything but eat. We went to Children's Hospital today to check on her diaphragm, etc. They said wait 3 more months and in the meantime, call an eating specialist. I pray she starts gaining weight faster and starts liking food.

September 25, 2000

I'm still consumed with my concern for Natania. It's hard to put into words. Her eating is still a concern. We saw a GI specialist today. He prescribed Pepcid AC for her and recommended some higher calorie Next Step Formula. She got sick several times. He said to continue with the Pepcid, but she's not eating at all, except the regular formula, and not much of that. He said the richer stuff may have been too rich. It's so difficult. I can't stop thinking that she is melting away. She's weak and it's hard. I thought once she was over the hurdle of her prematurity and her heart surgeries we wouldn't have the extreme ups and downs, but they never stopped for Natania. It breaks my heart. I wish I could do something to help her. Is it too much to want her to be healthy? It's a constant black cloud, and I pray God helps us and the doctors find answers. I pray every day she'll just "take off." With her being ill now, it's terrible to see her going downhill. I just love her so much.

Brialle is doing great. She shakes her head "no." It's so funny. Tim and I celebrated our 10-year anniversary. It was very nice.

October 26, 2000

Natania had a turn around! Right after her illness, she just took off and started eating everything in sight! She gained back the lost weight. They turned one, and Natania is 14.10 lbs., and Brialle is 18.9 lbs. They are doing great. Both pull themselves up on everything and Brialle can stand for a while without holding on to anything and Natania is just starting to stand for a couple of seconds. They are so sweet with how they crawl around together like they are on a little mission. They laugh at everything and are goofy. They think Kianna is so much fun and laugh at her all of the time. Kianna turned 5!

CHAPTER 15

SURPRISE!

NATANIA GREW STRONGER every day. Brialle was doing great. Doctors continued to be concerned with Natania's weight, however. We decided that it was too difficult to determine how many calories she was getting because she was still nursing, so we switched to formula only. With formula, we could increase the concentration to increase the calories. We just started doing this, and it was reassuring to know what she was getting. I felt a bit sad because I knew I was not producing as much breast milk as I needed to support twins. People tell you to take care of yourself, get rest, and eat properly, but this is impossible unless you have full-time help. If I had someone cooking meals, cleaning, and helping to care for the babies every day, it might have been possible. Anyone who has been in my shoes knows that just brushing your teeth is tough.

Knowing that the possibility of pregnancy can increase once nursing subsides, I discussed our options for the future with my doctor. I had always needed help regulating my cycles, and when combined with the need to let my body heal for a full year due to the C-section, we discussed having me try the birth control pill for a short time. The doctor gave me three months worth of samples to use when my cycle started.

I waited awhile, but nothing happened. In the midst of all of this, Natania's pediatrician sent us to have some further testing done, due to her slow weight gain. One test required an x-ray. I headed into the x-ray room with Tim, and the radiology technician asked if there was any chance I could be pregnant. I said, "Oh no, I'm sure I'm not," but Tim said that we didn't know that for sure. Just to be safe, he went in with her.

The next day, I was walking in the mall, pushing the twins in their stroller, with my friend Jody (Kianna was at pre-school). She had just learned she was pregnant and that her HCG levels were quite high. Her doctor mentioned that is what happens when women are carrying twins. She didn't want to get her hopes up, as it was very early. We were laughing about the possibility of her having twins too.

We decided to get something to eat at the food court. We settled on Chinese. After lunch, we were headed to the toy store to buy a gift for a child's birthday. As I stood at the checkout, all of a sudden I had this feeling that I was going to get sick—right there! I asked the clerk for a bag and took deep breaths. I didn't get sick, but I started wondering what had come over me.

That weekend, Tim suggested I buy a pregnancy test. I was nonchalant about it and decided to take the test when he was out. I was in complete (happy) shock when the test turned out positive. After so many years of struggles, surgeries, and pain, we had three beautiful little girls, and now I was pregnant with my fourth child! I was elated, laughing, and mostly in disbelief. As soon as I saw the result, the doorbell rang. It was my wonderful neighbor Ann, who had just baked some of our favorite cookies, and she was bringing a plate over to us. I must have been so out of it. I just remember my head spinning as I was trying to talk to her.

When she left, I wrapped up the test like a gift, knowing Tim would be home soon. He played with the girls when he got home, and I told him I had something for him. He unwrapped the gift, looked at it quizzically, then said, "What's this?" in a way that he may have had an idea. I said, "Guess!" He said, "No . . . really? Ha, ha . . . no, really?" I said, "Yes!" We just laughed and laughed. It was funny that after so many years of being childless, now when it rains it pours. It was truly unbelievable. I *was* "a woman who ended up with four kids."

God certainly had a plan. He may have known we might have stopped after three, but he made sure he sneaked the fourth in before we could stop him. We were delighted (and surprised).

August 6, 2000

I'm pregnant, again! What a shock! Wonderful, but shocking! We were going to start the pill the next cycle. I had prayed to God about it and said if was meant to be, now was the chance. Wow! The timing is good. I think this baby will be completely healthy.

August 29, 2000

Jody is pregnant with twins! Thank God! Please watch over her babies!

December 11, 2000

The ultrasound looked perfect! The baby was already 1.15 lbs. at 22 weeks, so it's over 2 lbs. now! The heart looked perfect according to the cardiologist! Thank the sweet Lord, once again! The baby is another girl. Four girls—wow! At least they think that is what it is. I'm so happy she is healthy and growing well! I'm excited about the thought that I may have a healthy baby that can come into my hospital room with me and come home with us! The whole concept seems new to me again. Kianna did, but that was so long ago. Kianna has been more delightful as she's getting more mature. She helps out so well with the twins.

January 6, 2001

27 weeks

Things are going well. Kianna has been out of school since Christmas; she loves playing with the girls. The girls are so much fun. They are both walking well now. So cute. Brialle says, "Baby" and "Hello," and is getting better about following simple directions. Natania helps get her clothes off for a bath and says, "Tickle, tickle" and "Hi, Dad." They both bark for "doggie."

Natania climbs on anything, Brialle follows. I caught both on top of the toy chest yesterday. Natania loves danger. If you say "no," she smiles and does it more! They love to dance. Kianna does the "Bulgarian Belly Blow" (as she calls it) on them (blowing on their tummies). Kianna sure has grown in the last year. Tall too! And beautiful. A little Cindy Crawford.

January 31, 2001

30 weeks

The baby is kicking as I write this. I'm looking forward to 3/27—the day they plan to do the C-section. I have to remember to enjoy and focus on our new baby so I can bond with her. I'm worried about leaving the twins while I'm in hospital. I think it's going to be hard on them—they won't understand. I'll miss them terribly, too! We are looking at building a house and are deciding on a builder. We could have built earlier, but it's good we waited since we never realized we'd need a home to accommodate 4 kids! We will have our hands full!

February 6, 2001

Sometimes things are pretty overwhelming. I just seem to shut down and lose my famous enthusiasm. Natania is a constant frustration with her eating. I wish I didn't have to be concerned about it so I could just enjoy her for a change—she is such a spirited little girl. She's adorable and knows it, but she is as demanding as 2–3 babies with her eating. Since she doesn't like to eat, I have to try 2–3 different "meals" with each meal. If someone else could feed her a bottle, it would really help. My sitters can't (Natania won't let them), and I don't want them stressing out about it.

I know we are up for a huge challenge when the new baby is born. I pray Natania starts to become easier. God, please help us know how to help her with eating and sleeping. Sleeping is a problem, too. She can't put herself to sleep, and we've been up a lot at night. With the new baby it will be very difficult. I pray this baby will be healthy and easy going. Brialle is a dolly—very easy, for the most part. Speaking of dolly, she doesn't go anywhere without hers. She feeds them, makes them talk, etc. Natania loves to play with Otis.

I was combining sleepless nights caring for the twins (they were eight months old when we learned I was expecting) with busy days with the babies and a preschooler, and being pregnant on top of that. Needless to say, I was a walking zombie. I thank God I have pictures and video, because sadly, I have little memory of those days. I look back and realize just how precious they all were.

The pregnancy went well. I admit, I let myself eat what I wanted—still reasonably healthy—but I gave in to my cravings. I think there is something to be said for that.

That's about all I remember. That's not a joke. I do remember loving the feeling (as with each of my pregnancies) of my baby moving around inside my body as she got bigger. When I felt movement, I knew the baby was OK, even though I was unable to focus on every little sensation as I did the first time around.

One thing I remember vividly. Natania and Brialle were old enough to be toddling around, and I was feeding Natania a new, high-calorie, vanilla-flavored shake. She was gobbling it down, and I was so thrilled with each ounce she took in. When she was finished, I went to the kitchen. All at once, she vomited all over the floor and me. I rushed to the sink to get something to clean it up, trying to keep Brialle and the dog away from it. Kianna was home too but in a different room. As I got back, still holding Natania in my arm, I saw Brialle getting closer to the mess. Since I wanted her to stay out of it, I rushed to clean it up. I had forgotten about a small area of vomit and stepped right in it with bare feet. The substance, as everyone knows, is very slippery, not to mention gross. Not only did I step, but I also slipped and fell hard, with Natania still in my arms.

Instinct made me put my elbow up, as I was carrying Natania in the crook of my left arm. Thankfully, my elbow and hip, not Natania's head, took the hard blow. I was focused on making sure she did not get hurt, yet I was very shaken up about the fall. Natania was crying, due to being scared, as was Brialle. Kianna came rushing in (I yelled to her to watch out for the mess) screaming and screaming because she thought mommy or her sister (or the baby in me) was hurt. Then the dog came running up and licked my face. It was pretty chaotic. And scary. Yes, indeed.

I handle emergencies by attempting to calm things down first, so I can evaluate the situation. When children are crying, you learn what the cries mean. Are they crying from fear, pain, tiredness, or hunger (or any other reason you can think of)? In this case, I knew Natania was OK, since I fell on my hip and elbow. I hoped the baby inside was also OK. I continued to tell the girls everything was OK, everyone was fine. I had all three in my arms, sitting on the floor, trying to calm them all.

After all of that, I cleaned up the mess. This time, I first put the twins in their gated play area and Otis outside. One never knows what excitement will happen in a day, does one?

February 13, 2001

Our little sweetie (the unborn one) is 32 weeks today. She is 4 lbs., 3 oz. and 38th percentile. Yes, it's confirmed, it's a girl. She's beautiful (ultrasound). I'm feeling great, overall. I need to eat better so she'll grow as much as possible. To think, Natania went home when she was 4 lbs! The girls are fine. Natania ate a little better today. They were chasing around in a play maze today, and they'd come out, run around the house, and both dive back into the play maze and giggle and giggle. They love books. Kianna has her Valentine's Day party tomorrow, so we made cut-out cookies.

March 3, 2001

At 34 weeks, our little baby was 5 lbs., 11 oz. Jumped to 61st percentile! Now I don't have to worry anymore! Eating more makes a big difference!

When I was about eight months pregnant, we knew we could not vacation too far from home, so we decided to take a trip in March to a place that had an inside water park in Wisconsin Dells. The twins were young, and it was a lot of work keeping track of them at that age (sixteen months), so my parents came along to help.

The day before we left, my mother stayed home with the girls while I headed to the maternity shop to get a swimsuit. Bless my father's heart, he offered to come along with me. When I wore the suit at the water park, I got a lot of looks. I'm assuming they were saying something like, "She looks like she's going to pop any second." I'm sure I did.

After a busy day of swimming and carrying sleeping babies all day, we went to a pizza place for supper. My body continued to tell me to take it easy. I could feel my belly getting tight, and I was having "Braxton Hicks" contractions. I knew I needed to lie down, but instead, I was trying to take care of the twins and Kianna. Even though my parents and Tim were there, when little ones get sleepy, they want Mommy. We convinced one girl to go with Daddy or Grandma.

We walked up to our hotel rooms. I was moving slowly and knew I had to lie down. Tim was due to go out of town that next day. He continually asked me if I was going to be OK. He planned to go that evening, as he had a commitment early the next morning. I assured him I'd be fine, I just needed to lie down and rest.

A few days later, I had a doctor's appointment to check how things were progressing. We had a scheduled C-section planned, and we wanted to be sure the date was still reasonable. Tim also planned to attend an annual business conference in Florida. He wanted to ask the doctor if it would be safe for him to go. If there was any chance of the baby coming early, Tim would cancel his business trip. After the ultrasound, the doctor assured him the baby wasn't coming anytime soon and things should be fine. Tim does not travel often, but March is a busy time for him. The baby came first, though. With the doctor's approval, I sent Tim off.

The evening he arrived in Florida, he told me he had gotten ill on the airplane. It sounded like the flu. Instead of attending the evening's events, he was ill in his hotel room. I felt bad for him and wished him well soon. Guess what happened next? In the middle of the night, one of the twins got sick in her crib. A half hour later, the other one got sick in her crib. My mother was staying with me, and she and I were up with them. I'm sure you can guess what happened next! Yep, now *I* was sick. So, now my mother was caring for the twins *and* me. I was able to take care of myself—rushing to the bathroom several times the remainder of the night—but I felt horrible that my mother had to be the one to take care of the twins. Kianna was OK. Whew.

Early in the morning, I noticed my belly was tightening up. Then it would stop, but about five minutes later, it would tighten up again, and then again. I was starting to feel a little better, but I mentioned my contractions to my mother. I found the entire situation to be quite humorous. I was almost "slap-happy." Mom convinced me that I might be in labor and should get to the hospital. My husband was in Florida, and I was here. I needed to get to the hospital, and Mom needed to care for the girls, so once again, my father stepped in, and he took me to the hospital. What a guy.

Sure enough, I was having regular contractions, but I was not dilating much. They assumed I was just dehydrated from the flu. Meanwhile, I was on the phone to Tim. He was still ill, but now waiting to learn if he should jump back on the plane home. He waited, and I waited with my father to see how things panned out. The nurses hooked me up to IV's and gave me something to slow the contractions, but nothing worked. We waited for the doctor to decide how we should proceed. I was exactly three weeks and a day early. Three weeks early (thirty-seven weeks) is considered "full term," so the baby should be fine. We decided to go ahead with the C-section.

Tim scrambled to find flights and jumped on the first plane back to Madison. He landed and headed straight to the hospital. We did not have a camera, clothing, or anything. The doctor and nurses waited until past midnight for him to arrive. As soon as he got to the hospital, they got him in his "scrubs" and rolled me into the operating room.

We didn't even have a chance to think of names for the baby.

Shortly after Tim's plane arrived in Madison, our beautiful fourth daughter was born. She was strong and vibrant and most importantly, she was healthy. She weighed 6 lbs., 15 ounces—our largest baby yet!

It was so comfortable the fourth time around. I felt like a pro. I loved having her to myself in the hospital. Holding her immediately was heaven. Tim also seemed like the experienced father and was so calm and happy.

She was a strong little nurser. From the moment she was born, I knew she was a spirited little girl. She knew what she wanted and that was that. I loved the fact that she ate well and was so healthy.

The day after she was born, we had a chance to finalize her name: Cailee Jean (after my mother). Things were good.

I was concerned about being away from the twins while I was in the hospital, mostly because of Natania's challenge with eating. It was such a concern that she had the stomach flu, since she cannot physically take going backwards as she did. She was not a big eater of solid foods, and I had to strategically plan her every bite.

Natania preferred healthier foods. If she had her choice, she would fill up on fruits and vegetables, so I had to offer the high-calorie foods first. What I did for her, had to be followed through with for her sisters too, since one would cry if the other didn't have the same thing. I laugh as I say this, because Tim and I were so adamant that our twins would have to learn to share and understand that not everything in life is fair. It's easier said than done, however, and the reality of foods—and toys for that matter—turned out quite differently. We ended up with two of everything (except the same books). Once our newest member of the family got a bit older, it was three or even four of everything (can't leave out big sister). Crazy.

I put together a detailed schedule toward the end of my pregnancy, so I was prepared for my mother or sitter to come in when I had the baby. I still had it in my computer, so I'm including it here. Reading it again, it is almost embarrassing how rigid and scheduled things were. It is funny to think how that was my life for a while! Natania had major eating aversions, and everything had to be "just so," and every calorie was precious. What a challenge for anyone to attempt to help out. I'm warning you, it's the real, unedited schedule.

Brialle and Natania Hanson

Schedule as of 1/1/01:

6:30am

Awake, change diaper. If they are just wet, no need to use wipes, but check if they need Desitin. After wipes, make sure they are dry before putting diaper on. (Use tissues to right of changing table, or use cloth on changing table). Leave pj's on until after morning nap, unless going somewhere.

6:45–7:00am

Breakfast. Wash hands. Start with baby fruit (pears, apricots, apple blueberry) Pour into bowl and use a separate spoon for each. If they try to grab spoon away from you, try giving them each another spoon to play with. Brialle eats well, Natania is not a great eater. Do not force Natania if she turns her head away and "swats" at spoon. Continue to feed Brialle and praise Brialle and continue to offer food to Natania periodically.

Next, offer something from "bread and milk" group. Brialle likes toast with anything on it (peanut butter, butter, jelly)—both might eat a toasted waffle from the freezer (break either up into small pieces and put on tray or plastic plate). Also offer Yogurt (put into dish, two spoons) or small pieces of a piece of Kraft singles cheese. Give sippy cups with ¼ juice and ¼ water.

205

7:30–8:45am   Playtime. They like to play in "playroom" on main level. They usually play well on their own—just make sure things they might try standing on are in the middle of room, in case they fall. At this time you might want to empty dishwasher, fold clothes, water plants, or vacuum/mop kitchen floor.

8:45am   Bottles. Feed at same time (Brialle feeds self, you feed Natania).

Brialle might take sippy cup (I'll let you know if/when you should start offering to her. Brialle drinks either a full sippy of warmed Vitamin D (whole) milk or 5 oz. in a bottle. Warm in microwave for about 30 seconds (when cold to begin with). Use curved bottle. Brialle can feed herself well, but you need to lay her back in her "boppy." She usually drains the bottle, but if there is some left, she will play and squirt it on floor, so take it away when she is finished.

Natania uses the straight bottles with the nipples with the "squiggle" on it. Fill with 7 oz. of HOT water—must be quite hot. Then add 4 ½ scoops of Next Step formula in cupboard. Shake well. When mixed, it totals roughly 7 ½ ounces of formula. She requires a "burp cloth" to suck on/play with before she may take the bottle. Just hand it to her, and when she starts sucking on burp cloth, bring bottle up and put in her mouth. While you hold the bottle, she will continue to play and inspect the burp cloth with her fingers; that gives her something to do. At this point, she'll probably just take some of the bottle to satisfy her hunger. She'll most likely want to wiggle out of your arms to play before she'll take the rest. By this time Brialle is probably done with her bottle and will play. Let them play till about 9:15am.

9:15am   Take Brialle up and put her in her crib (the one furthest away, under quilt on wall). She needs her "nunny" (blanket) you'll find in her crib (green satin-trimmed). She'll curl up in her crib with her blanket and put herself to sleep. If she fusses when you put her down, don't worry; she'll settle down. Take Natania's "nunny" with you when you leave the room. Push "play" on her remote control CD player for music (it is usually on the wicker stand to right of door or on dresser). Close the door.

This is when Natania takes the rest of her bottle. You'll need to re-warm her bottle in microwave for about 14–15 seconds, depending on how much is in it. It will be very warm. Sit in family room to feed her. If you are in their room, Brialle might not be asleep yet, and seeing you will get her excited again. Snuggle her in her blanket and offer her the burp cloth. When she starts to suck on her burp cloth again, offer the bottle as above. If she pushes bottle away, just let her suck on her cloth again for a little bit (few seconds) and offer bottle again. Bring bottle up under burp cloth and put bottle in her mouth so she can continue to inspect her burp cloth. She likes to be sung to or hummed to and rocked. She will go to sleep drinking the bottle. Keep bottle in her mouth until she pushes it away or turns her head. Don't worry about burping her until the very end. If she has not finished her bottle, put her burp cloth by her mouth to see if she'll start sucking it. If so, continue to try to put bottle in her mouth—if she does not respond to burp cloth, that means she's finished. It is very important she eat as much as possible, so you might try changing positions a bit just to rouse her, and then offer her the cloth again. Often she'll sleepily suck on cloth and drink a little more bottle. She won't take a cold bottle. Sometimes, if there is an interruption and delay and bottle gets cool, re-warm again (less time for less ounces).

Check to see if Brialle is sleeping on the TV/video monitor. On the TV remote, push the button below the ON/OFF button two times to have it come up. If she is sleeping, carry Natania up and lay her down on her side or tummy (she'll move to her tummy otherwise). If she wakes up a bit, just pat her back for a few seconds.

9:30–10:30am   While they sleep, please help around the house. Vacuuming does not wake them up as long as it isn't upstairs. Dust or do whatever you see needs to be done. Thank you!

10:30am   Time for them to wake up. This time may vary depending on when they actually went to sleep. I usually let them sleep for 1 hour. I'll let you know if there is a reason to let them sleep longer. Use video monitor to know what is going on. I usually turn volume way up so I can hear them wherever I am.

                 Take one out of her crib at a time—change their diapers and get them dressed, if they are not yet. When going downstairs, take one at a time. Lock upstairs gate when leaving that one upstairs while you bring other down. Lock downstairs gate when you go up to get the other. If the one you leave fusses, just tell her you are bringing so-and-so downstairs and you'll be right back.

10:45–11:00am   Playtime. In playroom or let them roam, with supervision, of course. Always make sure gate is locked going upstairs and door to basement is shut. They are walking quite well and do not usually get hurt when they lose their balance and plop on the floor.

12 noon   Lunch time. Wash their hands. Cook TV dinner in microwave or baloney/cheese or yogurt, etc. I will give you an idea of what to feed them

before I leave. They prefer to feed themselves. Cut noodles in half or in ½ inch pieces—make sure everything is in small bites. If cooking a messy dinner, try to feed them yourself first, with two different forks. Use bibs. They'll still get dirty. Offer sippy cups with ¼ juice and ¼ water.

12:45–1:30pm	Playtime. Sing, read books, go over colors, etc. They love musical toys.
1:30pm	Offer Brialle spill proof sippy cup (as above) and offer Natania her bottle (same directions as above). Lay Brialle back on boppy for her to feed herself. She might walk around with it. She might fuss that she wants a bottle. Don't worry if she does not drink all of it. Natania will take a break again; help Brialle with her cup.
2pm	Put Brialle in her crib as in AM. Give Natania remainder of bottle as in AM. Once Brialle is sleeping, put Natania in crib, when she's done and sleeping.
3:15pm	Wake and change diapers, then playtime.
5pm	Supper. Similar to lunch, I'll tell you what you can feed them. Kianna can eat now or later with you.
6:30pm	Bath time, if it is bath night.
7pm	Put on pajamas. Kianna too! T-shirt, cotton pjs, with sleeper over in winter, or T-shirt and pj's

only in warmer weather for babies. Kianna can pick out hers.

7:30–7:45pmish   Bottles: 7 oz. for Brialle, same as prior feedings for Natania.

Brialle can feed herself. Then she usually plays a bit.

Natania, again, takes some, plays, then at about 8pm, snuggle her up in blanket (give Brialle hers so she does not try to take Natania's). If you are by yourself, feed Natania in family room as Brialle plays in family room, rock and sing and turn down lights so she gets sleepy and takes bottle. If you have help, take Natania up to her room and rock her with low lights until she's asleep.

8:30pm   Or earlier if tired, rock Brialle and sing her to sleep. If alone, Kianna can watch cartoons, or if you have someone with you, Kianna should get ready for bed (brush teeth, go potty). Then other person can read Kianna 2 books max. in her room. Then Kianna says prayers and goes to bed. One of us usually lies next to her for a little bit. If you can't, tell her you need to go for now but you'll be back soon to check on her. If Brialle does not want to be held but seems tired, bring her to her room and either rock her there (as long as she's not being too loud so she does not wake up Natania) or try putting her in her crib with blanket and patting her back.

211

Nighttime:

Brialle usually sleeps through night. If she wakes up crying, WAIT—she will 95% of the time put herself back to sleep (Natania usually stays sleeping). If Natania does wake up, if she does not settle soon, take Natania out and close door. Brialle will get upset if she sees you, but she'll eventually settle down. Unless she is inconsolable for more than 10–15 minutes, don't go in or pick her up. If she continues, she might not feel well, and you'll need to evaluate it.

Natania usually wakes up 1–2 times for bottle. Ideally, 2am for 1 bottle only. Bring bottle up and keep in upstairs bathroom to prepare (formula is usually in cupboard in bathroom). Make 5 oz. hot tap water and 3 scoops. You can feed her in her room with nightlight. Brialle should sleep through. If she does wake and look at you, ignore her (never talk to them in the middle of night). She'll most likely go back to sleep. If she stands up and fusses, leave room with Natania and close door and feed Natania downstairs.

Other:

Dog:	1 cup dog food am; 1 cup pm; water always.
	If he barks, tell him no and put him in his "room" (bathroom downstairs).
	Keep door to laundry room closed; always and promptly put diapers away so he does not get into garbage. If he does, put him in his room. Let him out when he wants to or when he wakes, at lunch and before bed. He sleeps on our bed or wherever he wants (not in babies' room).

Medicine as needed:

Tylenol: Brialle—1 ½ droppers (use lines for measurement)

Natania—1 dropper

Decongestant—Brialle (see bottle, usually 1 ½ dropper)

Nebulizer: ½ container—put in bottom of nebulizer, above blue cone (you will need directions and training. We will tell you if Nebulizer is needed. Only use Tylenol with fever or if we tell you.

My mother and Tim needed to learn to work together as they cared for the girls while I was in the hospital. Like me, my mother is a strong woman. They both tried hard to respect each other's roles in my life. From laundry to what the girls were eating, they learned how to live with each other for a few days. It was endearing. Tim mentioned that the girls were eating quite a few hot dogs (and a couple laundry issues), while my mother mentioned something to me about laundry conflicts (and admitted how much the girls loved hot dogs). They were too cute together. I just let it go and felt blessed to have such a great husband and parents.

Kianna, Brialle, Natania, Daddy, Grandma, and Grandpa all came to see me and little Cailee in the hospital. When I looked at the twins, they seemed so small themselves—although they were big sisters now. Yet, at the same time, they looked big compared to their new baby sister. They also looked a bit "off," as their hair was not done like I would have done it—and Brialle had Natania's clothes on (so the pants were at her ankles), and Natania had Brialle's too-big clothes on . . . but that was OK. They were there, they were in one piece. They certainly got noticed by the hospital staff. Kianna also seemed like the experienced "been there, done that" big sister. She was used to handling babies and quickly held her new baby sister. It was like second nature to her.

Daddy introduces Cailee to sisters

Once home, the real fun began. Remember those sleepless nights? One would assume that by the age of seventeen months, the twins would be sleeping through the night, but they were up every night—one or both at least once, twice, or three times. When you combine this with a newborn sharing a room with Kianna and waking a couple of times a night, you can imagine the little bit of sleep we got.

Poor Kianna! She learned to pull her pillow over her ears when Cailee cried. She was colicky the first four months of her life, and let me tell you, she was the loudest of all my babies. I actually had to wear earplugs because of some minor damage to my right ear as a result of her screams.

My response to her screams was similar to the response to Brialle's monitor when it went off in the middle of the night. The only difference was I did not have to race Tim to get her. Cailee's cry was loud enough to wake everyone up, so the second she'd holler, I'd leap out of bed and bolt to her room to pick her up. If she woke her twin sisters, it was a mess. I tried hard not to wake Tim, since he had to get up in the morning and act like a "with it" adult with a brain. He could not afford sleepless nights.

When they were all awake, I nursed Cailee (or gave her a bottle with the same arm I held her in by twisting my wrist around to hold it) standing up, holding her in my left arm, while taking turns patting the twins' backs.

I would take turns patting one back for a few seconds, then went to the next one for a few seconds while "shh-shhing" them at the same time. This worked OK if they were fairly calm, but if they were standing up in their cribs hollering, then I went to "Plan B."

Plan B meant I took a twin out with one arm (holding Cailee with the other arm) and lay her on the floor, then I'd grab the other twin and set her on the floor too. I didn't put Cailee down because she would scream and make everything worse. Once all of them were out, I attempted to hold all three girls while I sat on the floor cross-legged. I tried to rock them and sing them back to sleep while I fed Cailee. Cailee was closest to my body. One twin lay up against my left leg, and the other twin lay on my right leg, maybe with my right arm around her. I continued this until all three fell asleep. Getting them all back in their cribs without waking them was another story. This was one of those times I wish I had a video camera going.

I've been asked many times how I managed, particularly at nighttime. I've now taken time to answer that question. I look back and am amazed at what needed to be done. I often wonder how in the world mothers of triplets or more do it. I am certainly not trying to promote how clever I was in all of this, although busier moms likely wouldn't have the time to write about it.

CHAPTER 16

GOD DOESN'T
FORGET THE
LITTLE CREATURES

IT IS AMAZING how different life is when you have a large family. Growing up with one older brother, things were pretty normal, and actually pretty quiet, as well. Adjusting to chaos and loudness was challenging. I still have difficulty with the loudness, although I'm learning how to be more efficient in an attempt to curb the chaos.

For example, I learned how much quicker and easier it is to have all my girls take a bath together. Everyone with multiple children likely already does this. When I only had one child, the thought of doing something like that seemed a bit undesirable. Now it saves time; I can dunk, wash, rinse, and dry them much more quickly. It is kind of an "assembly line" of bathing children. The water is not *that* dirty when they all come out. If

I want them to have some playtime, they have a lot of fun splashing around together.

Things that I needed regularly, such as diapers, socks, hair bows/barrettes, bibs, wipes, burp rags, etc., were kept in reach, particularly when I was rushing out the door. I kept these items on the main level so I could have quick access to them, either in the bathroom or laundry room off the garage, or—if I remembered to restock items—in a large diaper bag in the back of our vehicle.

I buy lots of white socks and shirts. While I cannot stand trying to match all of the white socks (I've actually had my friends Annie and Gail as well as my mother and mother-in-law helping me with those from time to time), at least I know they match everything. In fact, if they had disposable socks, like they have disposable diapers and bibs, I'd be happy. If I had time, I'd try to invent some. White shirts, although frowned upon by the girls' preschool teacher (she was always concerned about them getting dirty), are also smart, because they match everything and can be bleached. Pretty-colored shirts don't work because they stain and Shout is not "loud" enough for my kids' stains.

What else can I share that increases efficiency? Ah, yes, sunscreen. It takes *forever* to get the girls ready to go out in the sun. Have you tried the new spray-on sunscreen yet? I *love* it! It's quick and easy, although as I write this, I have one clogged in the sink. I'm still trying to figure out what went wrong there.

While all of these ideas helped me become more efficient and my intentions were certainly there, the consistency and follow-through were another thing. Most days our house was in a complete state of disarray—laundry piled high (either dirty, clean but in a laundry basket, or folded in a laundry basket), dishes always in the sink, toys everywhere. You name it. There was no "answer" to how to get it all done.

Getting around with four kids in tow.

Another element in this mix was managing our dog, Otis. No matter what I tried to help with life's efficiencies, when it came to the dog, the solutions to the challenges we faced were not always in his best interest.

Having a dog that barks every time you turn around does not mesh well with the science of getting three babies down for a nap. It never failed. If I got one or more girls down for naps, the dog would bark and wake them up again. When I was desperate for a nap, had cleaning to do, or was seeking a quiet opportunity to pay bills or make an appointment, I was not the most understanding person. I had nothing left to give when it came to Otis. He was a good dog, but again, the combination was a challenge.

The solution was to put the dog in his "room" (our bathroom in main level) when the girls napped. Between morning and afternoon naps, as well as the time it took to get them down, the dog spent a good deal of time in his room. He was not happy about it, but I really did not have a choice.

When the girls ate their meals and snacks, it also never failed: Otis always found a way to get up to their highchairs and get some food. When Kianna was not at preschool and was eating her food at the table, sure enough, as soon as I turned my back (to get their drinks or clean up or whatever was needed), Otis would get her food. I remember one time I was *very* hungry (and tired and crabby) and had two slices of bread left in the house to make myself a sandwich. I put the sandwich down on the table and realized I needed something to drink. When I got back to the table, it was gone, and the dog was licking his chops. Boy, was I mad! I was so hungry and there was little food left in the house and then the dog ate my lunch.

Another time, I had one girl in her highchair crying, another was on her potty seat in the bathroom off the kitchen screaming for me, the baby was crying, Kianna was calling for me, and the phone rang. Then the doorbell rang. Really, I'm not joking. I answered the phone to tell the person I would call back, answering the door at the same time. I was also yelling to the girls that Mommy would be right there to help them. I think it was a kid at the door. I don't remember, but I got rid of him. When I got back to the kitchen, the dog was *standing* on top of the table eating whatever food was left. I could have chosen to laugh at the situation or cry. I think I chose to cry that time. I was feeling overwhelmed.

Needless to say, it was now time for me to put Otis in his "room" when they had their meals and snacks. I felt bad for him, but I had no choice. Unfortunately, this meant that the dog was in his room a large chunk of time every day. He was not a happy camper, and I knew the poor little guy craved attention. I was physically and emotionally drained from caring for the girls, and I had nothing left for the dog. Before Cailee was born, I took Otis with me when I took the girls for a walk. After Cailee was born, I didn't have a triple stroller, so unless I had someone along to push her, I couldn't go. I tried the strap-on carrier, but after three or four attempts, one or more of the girls started screaming for one reason or another, and we'd only get as far as the neighbor's driveway. I gave up.

Where am I going with this? The dog started getting angry and jealous. When Kianna was born, he was wonderful and was great with her. She could have crawled up and taken a pork chop away from him (not that we gave him pork chops!), and he'd back away from the pork chop and let her have it. If he had an ear infection and she'd pull on his ears, he'd just whimper and take it. He was very protective of her from the moment we brought her home. But when three more babies came into the picture, he became more and more depressed about the lack of attention he received. When Tim came home, he was happy—there was another adult around to give him attention. Tim played with him and threw his toy for him and Otis was ecstatic—until the next day when Tim went to work again.

When Otis saw an opportunity to get something good, like food, he went for it—sometimes at the expense of the babies. He became challenging when it came to getting food. He acted like he deserved the food, since he got little else to make him happy. One time, he went for some food at the edge of the table at the same time Brialle did, biting her hand in the process. We thought it was an accident, discussed how serious it was, and eventually, we let it go. A few other times, he growled at the babies over food and acted aggressive toward them. He ran out of chances with me when he nipped Natania on the face as he attempted to get her sandwich from her. Luckily, the bite did not break the skin, but I did not trust him anymore.

I was raised believing animals are great, but they are still animals. People come first. You don't keep a dog that bites. I realize little children provoke and can cause the problems to begin with, but our children were too young to learn how to adjust their behavior around our dog.

I told Tim what happened and was adamant that we could not mess around; we needed to put Otis up for adoption. This was hard for Tim and Kianna. Tim never saw the aggressive behavior from Otis. Kianna rarely did. This made sense since their presence usually meant he got attention and was happy. Luckily for me, my parents also saw his aggressive behavior from time to time and confirmed that Otis behaved like that when they were around. This made sense because my mother was always busy helping me with the babies or with the house. She and my dad didn't give Otis very much attention when they were there.

Needless to say, I was feeling bad. I loved Otis and knew why he was acting this way. I knew he was unhappy. After talking to various sources, from the Humane Society to animal lovers, I was convinced we needed to let him go. I couldn't imagine him being in the environment of the Humane Society, so I checked around on adoption. I hoped I was making the right decision. It would be mine alone.

Within days of the biting incident, on an unusually warm day in mid-February, it was time for me to pick Kianna up from school. I got the little ones up from their nap and into the car, and actually took an extra moment to grab their shoes. So often I let them nap as long as possible and ended up running late. I'd get the girls in the car without shoes, expecting they wouldn't be getting out of the car anyway. This day I brought Otis with me as well.

While driving to school, I was struggling with my decision. I called Sara, the dear friend I used to work with at the TV station. If there was ever someone on the animal's side, it was her. She is a busy woman, but she happened to be at her desk when I called. I explained my situation to her. She knew how much I loved Otis, since we worked together during the time I got him. She also knew why we got him in the first place. She, too, thought it was best for him and for our family to put him up for adoption. She said she would pray that everything would work out. When we got off the phone, I prayed hard, asking God to guide us as I continued to drive to school.

After I picked up Kianna, the girls begged me to take them to Michael's Frozen Custard. Typically I would tell them it wouldn't work out, or I would just run in and get something from the outside pick-up window and bring it back to the car. This day, however, they had shoes in the car, they were appropriately dressed, awake, *and* the weather was beautiful. All of this meant that we went into the custard shop so the girls could get a treat.

As the girls were busy eating their treats, I noticed a lady come in with a group of girls. She seemed to know some other moms who were there and was chatting with them while the girls she was with got their treats. After a bit, the lady seemed to be watching my girls and finally asked if they were all mine. I told her they were, and when we discussed their ages, she learned I had twins. She was very excited and exclaimed that she, too, had four girls and her middle girls were twins, only they were all older. Her youngest was Kianna's age, her twins were seven, and her oldest was nine. As we talked about having a large family of girls, her daughters ran to the window "oohing and ahhing" over a dog that was walking by. The mother said something about the dog being cute and said something like "maybe someday" to her girls. All of a sudden it was as if God gave me a quick kick: "Here's your chance," and I said something like, "Oh, the girls like dogs? We have one that we are putting up for adoption." The woman said, "Oh, you're kidding! We're looking to adopt one!" It was too good to be true. She told me that they were going to get one for their oldest daughter's golden birthday (this is when the day of the month is the same as the person's birthday age). They'd gone to the Humane Society but hadn't had any luck yet. They had been looking for a smaller, non-shedding dog. Her daughter had her heart set on a dog that would be light or "golden" in color. They had been praying for the right dog for a long time. I know, too good to be true, right? I could not believe it.

I said, "You've got to be kidding! Our dog is smaller in size, non-shedding, and buff in color. And just half an hour ago I was praying that God would guide us in his adoption!" It was unreal. God even remembers pets.

Then I told her, "The dog just *happens* to be in our car right now, so you could meet him if you want to." She said they'd love to meet him! Her girls were squealing. Kianna was even excited about it. Next thing we knew, Otis was licking and jumping at them and wiggling all over as he ate up all the attention. I had tears in my eyes watching her girls with him. It was like they were meant to be together. My tears were tears of joy for him. Seeing him so happy was incredible.

Things were not all perfect, however. They were concerned about his age (he was eight), as they were hoping for a younger dog. They also preferred a female, but they fell in love with him from the start. All she needed was confirmation from her husband.

The timing could not have been better. We had been in the process of building the house, and we were moving into our new home that Saturday. Ideally, Otis would go directly to their home, rather than confuse him with our new home. I explained this to Heidi (the woman), and she agreed it would be best for Otis to adopt him before we moved. We had met them on a Wednesday, and her husband had Friday off, so they planned to come and let him meet Otis. If it was a go, they'd pick him up that day. It all happened so quickly.

Wouldn't you know it, the father and Otis bonded immediately. The dad joked about how maybe a male would be better for him, since he was surrounded by females. Seeing Otis with his new family was wonderful. They were an incredible family. Their daughters were so kind and well-mannered. I also noticed how kind hearted and calm the parents were. I knew it was the perfect family for Otis.

God handed them to us on a silver platter. They've kept in touch with us and let us visit Otis. Heidi told me how Otis would get into the garbage sometimes. Once, they had bacon for BLTs, and some bacon was in the garbage he got into. She lovingly explained to her daughters that Otis was simply following his instinct; he smelled something yummy and had to "hunt" it. Then they came up with a nickname for Otis: Otis: Bacon-hunter. It was too cute. When he used to get into *my* garbage, I was less than understanding. He would have simply ended up in his "room" again.

Heidi home schools her children and does a wonderful job with them. It was nice knowing Otis would not be alone all day long; in fact, Heidi told me the girls called him "Professor Otis," as he was always attentive and right by the girls' side when they were "in class."

We missed Otis, but we were happy for him. I also have to admit, it was a lot easier. No longer did I have to worry about keeping food and garbage away from him, feeling bad about keeping him in his room so much of the time.

Heidi and I both share the story often about how God brought Otis into their family. I believe that prayers are more easily answered when two sides are praying for the same goal. Never underestimate God's power!

CHAPTER 17

GAINING BACK
SOME CONFIDENCE

WHEN I WORKED before the twins were born, I put so much value in what I did in my career that I didn't feel I was doing enough at home. It seemed like I wanted to prove my value as a mother and a person. While Tim was working out in the real world every day, things were busy, yet still held some semblance of control. I felt bad when he came home after being around professionals each day who were well-groomed and could carry on an adult conversation to a home that looked like a tornado hit it and a wife who was crabby and exhausted and may not have showered. This was the life we learned to get used to for months (and years!) to come. We tried to remember, however, just how blessed we were despite our hectic life.

With four children, I thought life would be busy but wonderful. I figured I could handle just about anything fairly well. I tried hard to be the perfect mother and wife, although sometimes the harder I tried, the more miserably I failed. I believe I've finally learned the secret in my role. Most moms don't realize that it is abnormal to have things "perfect" when raising children. It's not only abnormal, it's impossible. Sure, there are some moms out there who might accomplish this, but it really depends on how things are structured at home, how much help they get from family members, and how many children they have. I've learned that attempting to reach perfection can have a negative result. Instead of focusing on the children, we instead focus on things that really don't matter (or shouldn't). Having the house look nice all the time (I secretly like the Pottery-Barn look and wish my house looked like the catalogs—mostly the "clean" part); making sure your children's clothes are matched, clean, and appropriate at all times; having your home "drop-in ready" so your unexpected visitor does not feel the need to call Social Services; making yourself look presentable at all times . . . the list goes on and on.

Our own level of expectations are hard enough to attain, but when you add the "experts" list of "should dos" that are impossible to achieve, it can be overwhelming. This list is even more insane than the expectations I mentioned above:

✓ Make sure you have three healthy meals and snacks that are in accordance to the pediatrics' recommendations (and don't forget—no juice or sweets between snacks).

✓ Apply sunscreen to the children even during winter months.

✓ Ensure that your children *always* say "please" and "thank you."

✓ Have your children always wash their hands before handling food.

✓ You should read to your children every day.

✓ Have one-on-one time with your child daily.

✓ Be sure your children have ten hours of sleep every night (dependent upon age).

✓ Teach your children to clean up after themselves (and be sure to constantly "manage" them to make sure this happens).

✓ Get your children outside every day so they can get fresh air and run free.

✓ Follow a consistent routine, as children enjoy knowing what to expect.

✓ Don't respond to your child when he or she whines or throws temper tantrums.

✓ Don't throw your own temper tantrum when your children throw theirs.

✓ Be consistent in how you discipline your children; stay calm and in control.

- ✓ Teach your children to use inside voices when they are inside.
- ✓ And, a biggie for me, ensure your children brush their teeth twice a day, floss daily, and use dental rinse before bed. The dental rinse is a battle for us. Every time they use it, they are suddenly dying of thirst, but drinking water after the rinse defeats the purpose!

You get the point. The list goes on forever.

From the outside looking in, we assume that all the other mothers can do it, so why can't I? When reading the list, it's impossible to accomplish *all* of these things every day.

The popular TV show, *Desperate Housewives* (as despicable as some of the characters are, some of the core challenges are true to some degree for many women), aired an episode where a mother of four kids was so stressed and tired that she started taking her son's medication—against her better judgment—just to stay alert and awake to meet the demands of being a wife and mother. She finally confessed to her friends what she was doing and told them how hard her job is. She asked them how they were able to do such a good job with their kids while she failed miserably. I've only seen the show a few times, but when I saw this episode, I cried. The other characters on the show hugged the woman and shared that they also had a hard time. And they didn't have four children like she did. They didn't know how anyone could do it. The mother just needed to know she was not alone and not a failure.

This reminds me a bit of something my mother-in-law said, "If all the babies are crying at the same time, just sit down and cry with them." It was funny, yet I realized it must mean it's OK to feel the need to do so. It made me realize that other moms in past generations have felt this way (and done this) before.

I remembered this advice from my mother-in-law during the times when I was at my wit's end with screaming and crying children and I needed to escape momentarily. I was not so out of control that I would have done anything crazy or dangerous; I simply tried to find a place to hide in the house to take a moment for myself and cry. Once, when all of the girls were out of control and inconsolable, I tried to do this in the bathroom. Unfortunately, they were onto me and followed me. Locking the door did not help; they all just started pounding on the door, screaming and crying all the louder.

My new hiding place was the pantry. They never found this one. It was in the back of the kitchen, and a sliding pocket door separated me from them just long enough to have a good cry and come back out a better mom. Did I feel guilty when Kianna called for me, wondering where I was? Yes, a little, but then I found a tissue to wipe my tears and blow my nose before I came out responding, "Yes, honey, what do you need?" Since she was older than the other girls, she might ask, "What's wrong, Mommy?" and I'd mumble something like, "Oh, nothing, honey, Mommy just had something in her eye."

Why did I share that? This is a slice of validation for readers who have been there, and my attempt to help other moms realize they are not alone.

A neighbor of mine once said something that helped me in all of this. Back when I only had Kianna, and achieving "perfection" seemed within reach, we were celebrating Kianna's birthday. The time to celebrate her party and dinner time got mixed together (maybe she fell asleep by the time dinner started and missed it). I contemplated letting her have cake so the guests could sing "Happy Birthday" to her. My neighbor said, "Diane, it's OK if she has cake for dinner; it's not going to hurt her." I remember looking at her quizzically and thinking, *Oh, OK!* She was someone who I always thought had it "all together," so hearing her say this made me feel a lot better.

Of course, the list I made earlier is only a list of recommendations. However, they can also make moms feel incompetent if they fail to accomplish them. Some other things not mentioned in my list are non-negotiable, like buckling the children in their car seats or holding their hands in a parking lot or not leaving your precious children in the hands of people you don't know well or trust. To me, as long as your children are safe, the other things can slide.

There are times that as babies they cry for so long and so hard that you can't take it. If you put them safely in their cribs and go out of the room to give yourself a break for a few minutes, it's OK. Experts say if new parents knew this, there would be less reports of shaken child syndrome. Parents need to know they cannot always control their babies' or children's behavior, but they can control how they handle it.

While I was learning all of these things, I realized that being a full-time mother was very challenging. It was the most difficult job I had ever had. I was thrilled to have our wonderful children and care for them every day, and I loved them more than anything in this world, yet the crying, whining, sleepless nights, and days filled with complete chaos were at times overwhelming to me. I longed for some control and appreciation.

I was raised to be independent, particularly from a financial perspective. I started babysitting at age eleven and worked all through high school waitressing; and I worked full time during college. I learned to work for everything I wanted and was grateful for the work ethic my parents taught me.

Wanting and needing are two very different things. My parents always made sure I had what I needed, including a college education. While my parents didn't care about designer clothes or fancy things, they did invest in my education. I know not everyone has that ability, and I am grateful for their hard work in sending me to college.

Raising our children, spending time with them, reading to them, hugging them—the list goes on and on—was great, although the laundry and cooking and cleaning I admit was a thankless job. Unfortunately, a large part of a mother's job is laundry and cooking and cleaning. I felt I did not go to college and do well in my career for L, C, & C. The longer I was out of my career, the less confident I became.

Tim was out experiencing new, challenging things every day, and I was hungry to use my brain as well. My lack of confidence was not helping our marriage either. Our common love of our careers and strong work ethic was one of the elements that brought us together in first place.

One day at church, my friend Annie mentioned a job she wanted me to consider in sales training. She said it was right up my alley and would be perfect for me. She had a solid understanding of my past career, since we'd worked together at two previous companies, most recently at the TV station where I recruited and trained her. She went on to explain I could work from home part time. It was a company I was familiar with. The speaker/trainer/owner put on a seminar for the station while I was in sales, and of all of the sales training I had personally been through, he was most in-sync with my philosophy.

I'm discussing this in my book because I know what I was feeling is normal for a lot of mothers. We love our children with a passion, yet we also desire to have an identity of our own. Maybe it's because I had a career for some time before having my children, and I got used to being mentally challenged. Being a stay-at-home mother is the greatest blessing on earth, when given the opportunity. And challenging it is. I've been blessed and would not give it up for anything. In considering Annie's offer, I knew that if I was to do anything with my career again, it would have to take a back seat to my first job of raising my children.

Annie knew this, but she also knew of my craving to be back in the business world. I was offered the position of Sales Training Coach for an international training organization, APEX Performance Systems. The agreement would allow me to work out of my home ten hours per week. The number of students I "coached" would determine the amount of hours I worked. Most of the contact with my students would be on-line, with minimal calls.

Tim was apprehensive about it. He said I couldn't even get done everything I needed to get done now, let alone work ten extra hours per week. He did realize how important this opportunity was for me, though. I had been feeling my confidence level slowly decline the longer I was not working. Although the timing might not have been ideal, as Cailee was not yet two, I was afraid this ideal opportunity might not come around again if I waited.

Yes, it was pretty chaotic. While I loved what I did and enjoyed training, it was difficult to juggle everything. I thought I could work while the girls were napping and after they went to bed at night, or early in the morning. Unfortunately, we put the twins into toddler beds about the same time I started my new job. So much for naps. Instead of napping, they would get out of control goofing around. Imagine having your best friend live with you every single day of your life. That's what it's like when you have twins sharing a room. No matter what I tried, or how much I threatened, they did not quietly rest. I gave up.

My best-laid plans did not work. I did manage to get my job done, but unfortunately, I continually struggled with separating my personal life from my work life. It worked best when I took a couple chunks of time to devote to my work and focused on the kids the rest of the time.

To help with this, I asked a babysitter to come in about ten hours each week. At first we had Cassidy, a wonderful young lady, and then Jill. I had someone helping on a fairly regular basis, even before I started my new position—for errands, grocery shopping, and appointments. While on occasion I brought *all* the girls with me, it took forever to get them ready and out the door. This involved getting them dressed, pottied, socked, shoed, brushed, snacked, and "coated" before we could go anywhere. It took a good twenty-five minutes. Getting them in their car seats took another six minutes. Getting them into a store took another five. Taking them along on an errand took at least twice as long as it did if I went alone. Then getting them all back in their car seats and home and "unpacked" added another ten minutes. I'm not joking. Ask anyone who has ever come along with me (although if I had someone coming along, I often begged them to sit in the car with the girls while I ran into the store alone).

When we got home, we'd *all* be wiped out. That meant the whining would start. The key time for whining children is what my friend Julie calls "the toddler colic hour" between about 5–6 p.m. It never failed. No wonder so many dads fear coming home from work. They walk into screaming and crying children and a crabby wife.

Thinking back, I realize just how doing anything was quite a feat.

It's funny when I see another mom with three or more children in tow. I find myself thinking, "Wow, she has her hands full!" Then I remember, "Wow, I have four myself. Is that how I look?"

Eventually, the girls started part-time preschool at Preschool of the Arts, the same wonderful facility Kianna attended. I was lucky not only to get them in, but also to get them all in on the same mornings. They went Monday, Wednesday, and Friday mornings from 8am–11am. It worked out nicely. When they were at preschool and Kianna was at school, I would squeeze in everything from meetings, conference calls, and errands, to even an occasional workout.

I continue to enjoy my job and have worked with many wonderful clients. I feel fulfilled in helping others in their careers, and it is great that our philosophy is based on ethical values.

While this was all fine and dandy, God wanted to make sure I didn't forget my commitment to him or to what is most important.

CHAPTER 18

NEVER TAKE LIFE FOR GRANTED

AUGUST 19, 2005, started out a bit hectic, I admit, as we prepared to travel out of town. I was unnerved. I had been busy with work and the kids, and we had been traveling a lot. The girls and I got home on Tuesday after attending my fraternal grandmother's funeral. While it was a very sad stretch of time dealing with her death, we were grateful God took her home. She had been suffering with dementia for several years, and she was miserable. When someone you love is suffering, you want what is best for him or her. After the funeral, Tim returned Wednesday evening after attending a business trip. I left the clean clothes in the suitcase and added more.

When Tim told me we needed to leave early in the morning, I was not thrilled. We had been rushing around, as usual. I got up really early so I could take a shower and get ready, as I knew I wouldn't have a chance later. We were headed first to the little cottage we'd bought, close to Tim's family. After stopping at the cottage, we were then going to head to Marquette, MI, for an annual "Ore to Shore" bike race. Kianna and Tim—and maybe the twins—were to be in it this year. Kianna was so excited; she had just gotten a new bike for an early birthday present and couldn't wait to try it out.

Tim was busy getting the bikes loaded on the back of the Suburban. We had recently bought a bike carrier that went on the back rather than on top. I was happy about that. Now we didn't have to worry about running into anything, like the roof over a fast-food drive-thru, like I had two years prior. Yeah, that was not good.

While getting ready that morning, for some reason, I felt compelled to paint my toe nails. All summer, I kept adding paint to my nails but didn't remove the old polish. We were planning to stay at a hotel that night. I knew we'd be swimming in the pool when we arrived, so I wanted to take the old stuff off and put on a fresh coat of nail polish. I also remember shaving my legs since I knew I wouldn't have time later.

Tim was frustrated with me. He wanted to be on the road by 6 a.m., although we didn't leave until 6:15 a.m. I typically like to have the house clean before we go out of town, and I'd stay up late the night before to do so.

This time I had a lot of work to catch up on, so I did that instead. The house was left in a state of disarray.

I was frantic and crazed before we left, but once we were on the road, I remember telling myself to "chill out" and that if I did, we might all enjoy ourselves.

Since Tim had just gotten back into town a couple of nights before from a business trip, he had not talked to his partner at work, so during the drive, he took the opportunity to tell him about the trip on his cell phone. He also made a quick call to his parents to tell them we would stop at our cottage for a while and to meet us there. He said his good-byes and told them we'd see them soon.

As our ride continued, the girls were drawing pictures and playing with their stuffed animals. We decided to stop at McDonalds for breakfast. We did the typical "eat in the car" thing. I passed food back to the girls.

During the drive, I happened to glance back at Cailee. I noticed the car seat strap that should be buckled across her chest was not where it should be. I told her to move it up so she would be safe.

That is the last thing I remember before I heard Tim scream and he violently swerved the Suburban. I saw a gray SUV coming straight for us—the other driver was going extremely fast. I couldn't believe what was happening. I heard a horrific crash—he hit us very hard—I was terrified. The next thing I knew we were completely out of control and flying through the air. Then we were rolling. I couldn't believe this was happening. I really thought this was it. We were going to die.

I had so many thoughts go through my head and heart and soul at the same time. I had heard the saying many times, but in an instant, I saw my life flash before my eyes. I felt so out of control, I thought, *I can't die because I have to be here for my babies*. I didn't know who would survive and who would die. I felt a paralyzing fear as I thought of losing a child, or more than one child. It was as if every ounce of life was immediately sucked from my body as I thought of losing a child. All the while Tim was yelling, "Diane! Diane!" I remember feeling his strong arm across me, even as we rolled and crashed around. I kept screaming, *"Oh, my God! Oh, my God! Oh, my God!"* over and over again.

When we finally stopped rolling and I knew Tim and I were alive, I let out a gut-wrenching scream: *"My babies!"* The absolute worst moment came in the next split second, as we paused before Tim and I turned around. We had no idea what we would see. It was terrifying. Our babies, whom we and so many others had prayed so hard for, whom we had been through so much with, and whom God had blessed us with . . . we had no idea what we would find. Tim knew where the SUV t-boned us. Our baby, Cailee, was sitting there. My mind didn't go there during the crash. I think it was God's way of shielding me. We turned around, and

I couldn't believe it. Cailee was conscious, and Kianna was too! Brialle was covered in blood; blood was gushing from her nose and above her eye, but she was alive! She sat up and said, "I'm OK, Mum." Just like our Brialle to know how I felt. We couldn't find Natania, however. I felt like my heart stopped. She was lodged between her car seat and the seat in front of her. I thought she was mangled up between the seats. Tim scrambled between our seats to get to her. I said a prayer and thought, *Not little Tonners. She's gone through so much in her life, not to die like this!* I couldn't bear the thought of *any* of our children dying.

Miraculously, Tim gently pulled Natania's car seat up. She was alive and in one piece. I cannot tell you just how incredibly grateful I was. Nothing else mattered—our babies were all alive. Thank God! I could not bear the loss of a child. My heart goes out to parents who have.

I took time to evaluate everyone's condition. I could see Cailee had a broken femur; her thigh was swelled up, and she was crying in a way that told me she was very frightened and in great pain. Considering she was the one who took the initial hit, I was incredibly grateful she was alive. It was miraculous, particularly considering the speed involved.

People quickly came to our aid. I was impressed by the kindness of all of these gentle strangers. They had such kind, concerned eyes. One man in his 30's looked like he was perhaps a hunter. He ran up to our vehicle and looked in with amazement. He said, "I'm shocked to see any survivors." It was too much for me to take in. We learned quickly that we needed to let the people help. Another man came up to Cailee's window. The windows had been broken out, and he just stood next to the vehicle, talking calmly to her. Everyone seemed taken aback by the fact that we were all alive, and they seemed so concerned for our little girls.

The man talking to Cailee told her how he had a little boy her age and kept telling her it was going to be OK. His concern was touching.

Another woman, I learned later, happened to be there that day by an act of God. She sat outside the vehicle with Natania and Kianna, reassuring them and talking to them. As a mother, I wanted to be there to calm and care for my children, but I couldn't be. The girls were in good hands. Tim was yelling for someone to bring something to stop Brialle's bleeding. Someone finally brought gauze and wrapped it around her head. She sat on the woman's lap, along with Natania, until the ambulance came. I later talked to this woman on the phone. She was driving right behind us and saw everything. She said she was supposed to be at work that day, but for some reason she was guided to take the day off and head north to enjoy the beautiful August day by herself. She knew when she helped us why she was not supposed to go to work that day. She said it was as though an angel guided her. She shared that with me before she even knew of our faith. It sent chills up both our spines.

I shared with her how we knew all our powerful angels were up in heaven to help us in the car that day. I told her my grandmother had passed away a few days before, and it was as if she knew she would be more help to us as an angel in heaven instead of sitting in a nursing home.

When things were somewhat in control, I did something that caused me to look down. I saw blood dripping from my head. I felt no pain, but I did not want the girls to worry, so I leaned over and pulled down the mirror from the shade. I had blood all over the side of my face from a decent-sized laceration on the left side of my head. I also had several cuts and scrapes and debris on the left side of my face. I knew I'd better do something to control the bleeding. As I attempted to find Kleenex somewhere (everything had been tossed and tumbled from the roll, and broken glass was everywhere) I noticed a large, dark stain on the seat where I had been sitting. I still did not feel any pain. It was scary, as I realized it was blood and it must be mine. I started to slowly check my body to try to find the source. As I got to my knees, I saw blood gushing from my knees and legs down to my feet. Some men saw this, as I had gotten into a position to view my legs. Tim told me to sit down because I was losing a lot of blood. He had such a look of concern on his face. He said I would go into shock if I didn't. One man could see I really didn't have any place to elevate my legs, so he offered to hold them up for me. Bless his heart. His only job was to hold my legs to help stop the bleeding. I was very grateful.

We heard the ambulances. The police and fire trucks were there. A guy, apparently from the ambulance, who was without a shirt (I heard he tried to get to us so fast he didn't have time to put one on), tried to analyze the situation. I was very "with it," as my motherly instinct told me to be as alert as possible. As they asked questions, I wanted them to know my head injury was not that bad and I knew what was going on.

Two ambulances came for us, and one came for the man who caused the accident. I couldn't see the guy, but I looked up the hill on the road and saw a gray Dodge Durango that was smashed in on the right front. We somehow ended up a long way from him, down a hill. The woman who was a witness later told me he hit us so hard that we spun up into the air like a tornado; then we crashed down on my corner and rolled (I don't know how many times).

At one point I heard Tim say, "Where's the guy who hit us? Where is he!?" Everyone seemed to understand. By that point, the police were talking to the man—Tim was so focused on helping his family, he didn't think about the person or cause until that moment. Part of me wished he could have screamed at the man to make him realize that he almost killed his family. It took a lot for Tim to let it go and continue to focus on us.

When I looked at the Suburban, as the medical staff was getting me into the ambulance on the stretcher, I was impressed at how well it held up, considering the severity of the accident. It maintained the frame structure, with the exception of the initial side impact and slight crunching on the corner where I sat. Back when we were deciding on what vehicle we should have for our family, I remembered the story of the family driving the mini van and how their children were killed. It gave me chills again to realize how lucky we were to have this vehicle in this kind of accident.

It took a long time to get everyone into the ambulance and head to the hospital. Everyone but Natania and Kianna was on a stretcher. There was talk of Natania and Kianna riding separately in a police car. That was the last thing Tim and I wanted. We convinced them to let Kianna ride with Tim and Cailee, and Natania ride with me and Brialle.

During this, a man had a bag/purse. He described it to me, asking if it was something I needed. I told him it was my purse. He said he would put it in the cab of the ambulance. Before we left, some attendants were rushing around trying to locate "the woman's purse." I lay there and tried to tell them where it was. I continued to try to get their attention to tell them it was already in the ambulance. They finally heard me, but I got the impression they did not want to heed much of what I said because of my head injury. They eventually found my purse.

I had a neck brace on, so I couldn't easily turn my head. I continued to talk to Brialle so she would stay alert because of her head injury. I was scared about the severity of it. I couldn't see her since the neck brace prevented this, but I continued to talk to her and reached out to hold her hand. With my other hand, I reached for Natania. She was sitting on my other side, on the seat next to my stretcher. Brialle was afraid, so I continued to talk to her and reassure her.

The ambulance personnel were wonderful. At one point, both Brialle and I needed oxygen. I felt myself become light headed. I started to worry about the blood loss we had both suffered, and I wanted to be alert for the girls.

The sound of the ambulances and sirens was surreal. We always pray for people who need ambulances, and now we wondered if someone was doing the same for us. Whenever I hear sirens now, I *feel* what the person(s) is (are) going through.

While we were being transported to St. Vincent Hospital in Green Bay, I asked the ambulance personnel for my cell phone. I called my parents, and my father answered. I said, "Dad, we've been in a very bad accident, but we are all alive." He panicked, and I continued to tell him we were all OK. I remember telling him how scared I was for my babies. I could feel the emotion from him through the phone lines. He said, "I need to find your mother. We'll be there as soon as we can. I'm so glad you're OK. I love you." I then called Jennifer. Jennifer said, "Honey, I am so glad you are OK. Be sure everyone gets checked out from head to toe, and request an MRI for everyone, just to be safe. I love you." I also called Melissa, our friend and godmother to Brialle. Tim called his parents, and his mother was so upset. He had to keep reminding her we were all alive, as he could hear her crying. I heard him say, "Mom, it's OK, we're

OK. We are all alive, and that's all that matters; mom, it's OK, it's OK . . ."

The scene at the hospital was like something out of a TV show. Multiple trauma teams had been called into action. There was a lot of hustle and bustle as doctors directed us to specific rooms, nurses began taking new vitals, and all were shouting orders and asking us questions. I remember trying to appear "with it" so they would listen to me. I told them how many were in our family, and told them how we wanted to be together. Still on the stretcher, I couldn't see anything very well from a lying-flat position. They told me where I was. I was put into a room with Cailee and Brialle. I had not seen Cailee since she was taken from our vehicle, still strapped into her car seat to keep her immobile. They said, "She's OK. She is sleeping now, we've sedated her." I got a glimpse of my baby and wanted to be there for her, but she was sleeping. I wanted to hold her, but I couldn't move. The feeling of wanting to hold and comfort your child but not being able to was so hard. For this reason, I am again reminded how grateful I am for the woman who helped us by being with the girls.

People came in and out. The initial evaluation included cutting off our clothing. I told them I was fine and I could take off my clothing (at least my upper half). I told them I had been moving since immediately following the accident. They insisted I not move and proceeded to cut off my top and favorite bra. Often accident victims don't even realize they are hurt, they said.

We were in the emergency room for several hours. They brought in x-ray machines, and many doctors came in and out. When they finally let me out of the neck brace and allowed me to sit up, I was able to look at my legs for the first time. They had started to hurt more as time passed. I was shocked at their appearance. It was as if someone had taken razor blades to my knees. They were sliced open, and although a lot of the bleeding had stopped by then, I saw a lot of dirt and debris, and even some grass that had been forced into each laceration. Dried blood covered my legs and feet. I finally asked for a mirror to see my face. As I inspected it, I saw the large laceration next to a mole I have on the left side of my head, and how my hair was hard with dried blood. My eyelashes were missing from my left eye —that was how close I had come to losing my eye. There appeared to be small cuts all over my eye and left side of my face/ cheek. It was hard to differentiate between actual cuts or lacerations, debris, and dried blood.

The hardest part about my care was cleaning out my lacerations. A woman started to "scrub" my face, and it really hurt. She didn't know if there was glass mixed with the blood and debris. It felt like she was doing more damage. I'd learned to be an advocate for myself and told her to please stop. Then I told her what I wanted or needed her to do. I told her to please soak my face with saturated cloths first, to loosen the blood. She went along with it. She was very kind. Another woman attempted to clean my legs and feet. As she washed my feet, there were my red-painted toe nails. As she started moving higher up my legs, she could see we had quite a job on our hands. I offered to help and asked again for towels and lots of sanitized water to pour on my legs.

In the other rooms, they were running tests on the others. Kianna had complained of a headache, so they ran a cat-scan. At the accident scene, Tim was running around, trying to help all of the kids. Once the ambulances arrived and everybody was stabilized, he complained of a sore neck. They immediately strapped him to a back board and wouldn't let him move, and now the doctors were performing x-rays and cat-scans to check him out. Like me, they had to cut off all of his clothes. Tim wears a crucifix necklace. They normally cut off all jewelry and do not allow it during x-rays of the head or neck. But once they saw it was a crucifix, they decided to leave it on. What a comfort it was to know we had been transferred to a faith-based hospital and the doctors and nurses respected that.

In addition to Brialle and me, Cailee was in serious condition with her broken leg. She needed surgery to repair it. They decided to surgically implant a steel rod through her hip and attach it to her knee to stabilize her leg. She would then have another surgery once her leg healed to remove the rod. The orthopedic surgeon was very nice and seemed well qualified for adults, but he did not specialize in pediatric patients. He had done very few procedures like this on a four-year old like Cailee. Tim and I have a wonderful family acquaintance with a pediatric orthopedic specialist at U.W. Hospital in Madison. Dr. Noonan is one of the best in his field and also is one of the nicest doctors we know. We discussed with the emergency room staff the pros and cons of transferring Cailee back to Madison to have the surgery. After discussing whether she could be stabilized for the trip, who would transfer her, and the follow-up care she would need, the doctors agreed. U.W. Hospital agreed to accept her, so they started planning her transfer.

Other than bruising and soreness, the tests on Tim's head, neck, and back came back without serious problems, and Kianna checked out fine as well. For the time being, Natania checked out fine as well, but that would change later on. At least for now, things were under control.

Meanwhile, family started to arrive. The looks on their faces told me they had cried their tears and now tried to stay strong. I tried to stay strong to reassure them that we would all be OK. They looked at my legs almost with disgust; they were feeling bad for me. I tried to make jokes and assured them I was OK. I could tell they were not only just concerned about my physical well being, but also my mental well being. They knew how I felt about what happened to my children—their grandchildren and nieces.

When your child is hurt, the first instinct as a parent is to be by his or her side. In our case, with four children and with my injuries, it was not possible. Tim planned to stay with Cailee and accompany her in the ambulance to be transferred back to Madison. We asked if Brialle and I could be treated in Madison, but were told "no" due to the increased chance of infection.

Brialle had serious and deep facial lacerations around her eye. Because she could be permanently scarred, and they were concerned about the wounds affecting her facial expressions, I wanted to be sure we had a good plastic surgeon. They originally discussed stitching us up in the emergency room, but after we discussed a plastic surgeon, they agreed.

After a while, the plastic surgeon came in. He seemed a bit arrogant. I wanted him to see us as real people and wanted him to do his best and found myself attempting to befriend him. This may seem a bit odd, but when someone lets themselves feel for the one(s) they are caring for, I believe they try harder and see the importance of what they are doing, rather than just doing their job.

I shared with him what had happened in the accident and that we were innocent victims and what our little girls had gone through. I started asking questions about his life and family. He worked on fixing me up for quite a while, so chatting seemed like the thing to do. I learned he was married and had young children too. After a bit of time passed, he started treating me with kindness.

When the doctor began working on me, my mother stayed for a while to hold my hand. The injections he gave me were not only excruciating, but I started feeling strange as well. My heart raced, and I felt like I was having a hard time breathing. I tried to explain this to the doctor, but he continued to reassure me the injections should not be a problem. As he continued to numb my legs in various areas, the pain was so great that my mother just squeezed my hand hard and continued to stay with me.

Before Tim left with Cailee, and while I was still being stitched up, he came in to be with me. My mother left so we could be alone, although the doctor was still working on me. This was the first time since the accident Tim and I were actually together. Just seeing him made me break down when he held me in his arms. I sobbed uncontrollably and loudly while he held me. I kept telling him how scared I was and how I thank God for saving our little angels and us. It seemed impossible that we were spared in such a bad accident. The doctor graciously continued to stitch me up and seemed to try to give us our space.

My sister-in-law Chrissy also came in to stay by my side. She had no desire to see what the doctor was doing; she focused on my upper half and looked at my face while we talked. We talked about how her late husband,

Mike, who died at the young age of thirty-seven, was one of the angels who helped us survive. Her husband was a police officer in Green Bay for many years. He also spent a lot of time volunteering for great causes, including organizations his two daughters were involved in. We all knew he would have done anything to save us as an angel in heaven; that was just the kind of guy he was. It was a blessing to know he was watching over us. It's so hard to explain this to someone who has not experienced this, but we just knew he was.

Chrissy was there for the remainder of the evening. She had a friend who was at the hospital that evening for a severe asthma attack, so she went between rooms, being there for both of us.

When the doctor finished up with me (about 200 stitches later), he had to take care of Brialle's lacerations to her face. The injections of the numbing solution in my face had been more painful than my legs. I wanted to be there for Brialle because I knew it would hurt her. I am forever grateful that, once again, my mother could be there for her. I told my mom she had to deliver a very important "message" to Brialle from Mommy. I told her to tell Brialle, "Mommy said it will hurt when the doctor has to give you some 'pokes,' but only for a few moments, and then the pain will stop. For each 'poke,' count to ten and the pain will have stopped, but be sure to hold *very* still."

My mother knew how important it was for me to share this with Brialle. Mothers know their children, and I knew if Brialle knew what to expect, she would be a big girl and get through it. Various family members came in to give me updates. My dear mother-in-law, my father, and my sister-in-law Melanie all checked in with me to let me know how Brialle was doing. They all were also spending time with Natania and Kianna, reassuring them and being there for them. Everyone's love and support was overwhelming.

Tim had also been talking to the hospital chaplain. The woman was so kind and offered to contact our church in Madison. Soon, we had the pastors and congregation talking and praying. It brought back memories of when Natania was fighting for her life. Despite the horrible accident, I felt as if we were all enveloped in love and gentleness.

When they finished with Brialle, another family member stayed with her while Mom came in to let me know how Brialle had done. Brialle had a deep puncture wound on the inside corner under her eyebrow, and Mom was concerned if the doctor would be able to "close" it, but he did. She was very pleased with his work (in her career as an RN, she spent many hours observing in emergency room surgery). It took twelve stitches to get her patched up. I was elated that it went well for Brialle, and again thanked my mother for being there with my little girl.

Once things calmed down, we started to ponder, "What next? How do we get home?" My sister-in-law Melanie thought to bring her Suburban down from Kingsford, planning ahead to drive the rest of us home. The next thought I had was that we needed new car seats for the girls. I asked my parents if they wouldn't mind going to the local Wal-Mart to find three car seat/booster combinations.

My parents left and came back with the car seats. They had to juggle getting them into Melanie's vehicle, and they wanted to make sure they were installing them just as Daddy would have. It took awhile, but they were finally ready. It gets a bit fuzzy after this. I believe I was being discharged and Chrissy was pushing me in the wheelchair. Melanie had Natania, Brialle, and Kianna with her. We were meeting my parents in the lobby once the car seats were safely buckled in. As we waited, I decided to call Melissa on my cell phone to give her an update. As I was talking, I recall getting very, *very* tired. I started slurring my words, and all at once, I fainted. Natania was right there at the time.

The next thing I remembered, I felt my hair "blowing" in the wind as I was rushed back down to the nurses' station, and I could hear Melanie's voice shouting my name. Melanie is a very strong, respected mother, and I knew by the tone in her voice that she meant business. She was concerned and trying to (gently) slap me on my face to get me to come too. I did.

After all this, I was re-admitted. The nurses and doctors joked with me and said I must really like them. They were trying to figure out why I had passed out. I assured them I'd be fine, I was likely a bit anemic and dehydrated after losing a lot of blood. They hooked me up to an IV to pump fluids in me.

Meanwhile, the rest of the family was hungry. Realizing the girls had not eaten since we stopped at McDonalds for the Egg McMuffins at 9:30 a.m., I encouraged them to go out to eat and that I would be fine. Chrissy, however, decided to stay with me. She was very thoughtful. She continued to check on her friend and me. When it was time for me to be discharged again, she asked me if I was hungry and wheeled me to the vending machine in the lobby, where she bought me some pretzels and water. I was not hungry, but she encouraged me to get something into my stomach.

When everyone came back from getting something to eat, they met me in the lobby. It was difficult to get into a vehicle again. Melanie was going to drive us home in *her* Suburban. It was hard for the girls to be passengers too. I felt tense and prayed we'd get home safely. We were to follow my parents home, and everyone was preoccupied. After a couple of wrong turns, we headed home.

Melanie had stopped for gas half way through our trip home. My parents stopped too, and my mother came over to see how I was doing. After all of the fluids the hospital staff pumped me up with, I had to use the restroom. What a sight I was! I had bandages on my legs and head like a mummy, and my hair was still saturated with hard, dried blood. Needless to say, I drew some attention as my mother escorted me gingerly to the restroom.

We finally reached home. I had warned Melanie that we left our house in a state of disarray that morning. I was embarrassed to have family see the mess we left, since typically I try hard to "tidy up" so we have a clean home to return to.

When we walked in the door, I looked at the kitchen island, and there was the obituary "card" with a photo of my grandmother who had just passed away. Her photo got my attention. She had suffered in her last years, and it was as if she was saying, "I was not able to do much for you on earth, but in heaven, I could be your guardian angel when you really needed me." Seeing it warmed my heart and brought tears to my eyes.

Melanie and my mother assured me our house was not that bad as they rushed around (picture two very efficient women determined to whip everything back into shape). I was pretty much useless. It hurt to stand and walk, but I wanted to do as much as I could for the twins so they could still have Mommy get them to bed.

My mother and Melanie offered several times to put the girls to bed, but I was so thankful they were all alive, I just wanted to be with them and assure them everything would be OK. They helped the girls with their PJs and brushing their teeth. We put a mattress on the floor between the twins' beds for me to sleep on, so I could be with them that night.

When I woke in the middle of the night needing to use the restroom and take my medications/pain killers, I didn't want to wake the girls, so I went back into my bedroom, where my mother was sleeping and where our bathroom was. Getting up from the mattress on the floor was excruciating. I couldn't bend my knees, and getting up from a mattress on the floor without bending your knees is next to impossible. I almost fainted as I started my trek to my bathroom. A couple of times I had to stop and bend over to get the blood back to my head. I also thought about Tim at the hospital with Cailee, wondering what was going on. My mother was sleeping in my bed in case I needed her, but I couldn't convince myself to wake her; she'd been through so much herself, and she needed her rest. Somehow I managed to get back to the mattress and carefully maneuver myself into it. The girls stirred a couple of times, but fell back to sleep when I verbally comforted them.

The next morning, I was eager to see Cailee. Tim had a rough time once she was transferred to Madison. He was tired and concerned for his family, while dealing with problems in getting proper care. U.W. Hospital is a Level One trauma hospital, which means it receives all kinds of life-threatening emergencies. It was a Friday night, and it was very busy. Since Cailee had been stabilized, other patients could delay her surgery. Indeed, they did. After several false-starts throughout the night, they delayed her surgery until morning. As I mentioned earlier, we requested U.W. Hospital because we knew the pediatric orthopedic specialist, Dr. Noonan. Unfortunately, he was traveling on vacation and not available when we arrived. In the meantime, we worked with his associates, who were very capable.

I do not recall how I got to the hospital to see Cailee. Either my father or Melanie drove. They needed a wheelchair for me, and they rolled me as far as they could go so I could see Cailee. Tim took over and brought me to our baby.

When I saw Cailee, she was still sleeping. She was in a full body cast (bright pink!) up to her chest. It was open at the bottom so she could go to the bathroom. She looked so precious and sweet. It killed me that I couldn't scoop her up in my arms and hold her. Tim explained everything to me. He had stayed by her side the entire time. The doctors decided she did not need to have a steel rod inserted in her leg. Although the body cast was more difficult for a few weeks, she would be much better off in the long run, as she wouldn't have scars from the surgery, pain from the rod, and likely arthritis from the foreign object. I was grateful Tim was there through the whole process and thankful we made the decision to transfer her to Madison.

I was concerned about Tim, as he was in pain of his own. At one point, he finally shared that he thought he had broken ribs, but never once did he ask to be checked out further. He was too busy caring for his family and was concerned he wouldn't be able to stay with Cailee.

When Cailee finally awoke, she called me. She couldn't move anything except her arms, head, and from her right knee down. I talked softly to her and told her I loved her and held her hand. I tried to give her an "upper body hug," but with the big cast, it was difficult. What amazed me was how she was such a big girl about everything.

Using the bathroom would be a challenge for her. She needed to be carried and strategically placed on the toilet. It was challenging, but she accomplished it and didn't complain.

I went home later that morning so I could rest. I could not do much at all, except keep my legs elevated and answer the phone calls from concerned friends and family. My mother and sister-in-law did so much to help. My mother and father-in-law also came to help when Melanie had to leave. They were wonderful.

That evening, I ached to see Cailee again. When I got to the hospital (my father took me), the nurse asked if I wanted to hold her. I was so happy. It was difficult because I had to keep my legs elevated. They got in the way as I tried to keep Cailee's heavy body cast from scraping at them, but Tim and the nurse gently hoisted her up onto my lap as I sat in a glider rocker. She was so heavy with the body cast, but it was heaven to hold her. I snuggled up to her and sang to her and didn't want to put her down. When my circulation began to cut off after a while, I had to ask them to put her back into her bed. Tim did a wonderful job trying to reassure her that Mommy needed to rest too, but that I was right there by her side.

The next morning, I went back with all of the girls to see Cailee. Our friends Kevin and Melissa came too. Kevin's parents were on their way down from the Iron Mountain, MI, area to Madison on the day of our accident to visit. They had heard of a nasty accident on the highway. They were very upset to hear it was our family. People who witnessed the accident or were driving by or stuck in traffic as a result had a lot to say about what they *thought* had happened. It was rumored that there was at least one death. It is surreal when you think that they were speculating about *our* family.

That same day, Cailee was released from the hospital. Tim's parents were with the rest of the girls, and everyone was overjoyed to see her. We had a child-sized wheelchair delivered for Cailee to use, although she became upset and refused to use it. (We later learned that Cailee thought the wheelchair meant she would need to use it for the rest of her life.) Cailee was somehow able to fit into her old "umbrella" stroller, even with the big bulky cast, and chose that to get around. Her sisters, however, found it fun to use the wheelchair (good thing it was used for something!).

Natania was crawling around on the floor, pretending to be an animal, when suddenly she started screaming and crying that her shoulder hurt. She had a hard time moving her arm, and when I looked at her shoulder, it looked like something was off. She had complained about it hurting a little since the accident, but it also appeared to be bruised, so I didn't give it much more thought.

Although we were only home a few minutes after Cailee was discharged, we headed back to the emergency room for Natania. This time we chose St. Mary's Hospital, since that is our typical hospital. Luckily, Natania was able to get in quickly. They knew she needed an x-ray, and it would be easy to determine what was going on. Sure enough, her x-ray showed that her collarbone was broken. It was snapped just like a twig. They said the accident must have broken it, but not all the way. When she moved a certain way, it snapped the rest of the way. It was very painful for her.

The doctor explained there was little that could be done for a broken collarbone except to have her wear a sling. She could not move her arm up at all, and any slight bump was very painful.

Friends and relatives and our church family were so incredible during all of this. It was overwhelming how many people were impacted by our accident. So many people love our girls, and many have children. They put themselves in our situation as mothers and fathers and grandparents. We had wonderful friends and neighbors who helped in so many ways. Many babysat while we attended numerous doctors' appointments. Tim's coworkers arranged for weeks' worth of meals and sent gifts for the kids. Clients of mine and Tim's from across the country heard of our accident and sent gifts. Annie, Gail, Tiffany, Kevin and Melissa, Stacey, and Lisa from church, and so many others, made meals. We even awakened one morning shortly after the accident to our neighbor, Jim, mowing the lawn. Everybody wanted to help in any way they could.

Some of our friends from church, Stacey and her husband, Tom, and Lisa and her husband, Mike, told us how shaken they were upon hearing the news. They all knew our family and our daughters well and have children the same age as ours. When I put myself in their shoes and thought for a moment what I'd feel if they had experienced the same situation, I shuttered. I love their children and have spent a lot of time with them. We teach each other's kids in Sunday school and got to know each of them on an individual basis. I would never want them to experience the same kind of horror that we experienced.

They say God only gives you what you can handle, and we were certainly pushed to the limit to get through every day. The first few days after the accident I was unable to be alone with Cailee for any length of time because I was not able to lift her. If she had to use the bathroom, I needed some help.

School started about a week after our accident. I contacted the school to ask what they could suggest for Cailee. They were very concerned about our family (when they heard the news, they sent over a big bunch of balloons for the girls), but they admitted they could not handle Cailee in her situation. The Christian school that the girls attend could not fund special teachers to help special-needs children like Cailee. I got a taste of what families go through who have a child in a wheelchair long-term or permanently. I am familiar with how my parents handled my brother's developmental disabilities, but after this experience, I often think of the challenges other parents have to deal with every single day. I always try to remember not to complain and to realize someone else has it worse off. I know that families who care for their special-needs children round-the-clock are the ones who deserve a gold medal. They are my heroes, in addition to the children themselves.

Shortly after our accident, I informed my employer that I needed to take a family leave to care for Cailee. Part of this meant I would go to school with Cailee to attend to her needs.

It took some creative planning. It started with getting up early in the morning. I showered and changed the dressings on my legs, then put Brialle's antibiotic cream on her eye and massaged it for a few minutes, to help prevent scarring. Then I'd help Natania get dressed so her arm/shoulder would not hurt. After the twins were situated, Tim would take Cailee to the bathroom and we'd get her changed. The only thing that fit over her body cast was a wide-skirted dress; we found some long-sleeve cotton ones from Land's End that would act as her school uniform for the next few weeks. Finally, Tim would carry Cailee into our new Suburban (we *know* it is one safe vehicle!) before he went to work. When we got to school, I met a friend in the school parking lot to help get her out. My friend Adrienne, the mother of Natania and Brialle's friend Anika, was more than willing to help me.

Cailee got out of school at 11 a.m., and I attempted to get someone's help to put her back in the vehicle. This continued only a few days, as I was eager to be independent and help my own child. I did not like all of the attention. I probably started lifting her sooner than I should have, but I did learn how to leverage her to take pressure off my back. As long as I did this without bumping my legs, I was fine. When I bumped my legs with her rough cast, it was not fun.

I picked up the rest of the girls at 2:35 p.m. This meant I either needed to hoist Cailee back into the car to get them (and back into the house when we got home) *or* get someone to help me load her up and take her back out upon our return, like a neighbor, *or* have someone stay with Cailee while I picked up my other girls. My dear neighbor, Tiffany, kindly offered to stay with Cailee a few times a week. She was a life-saver.

Tiffany, her husband, Dan, and daughter, Ava (age eighteen months at the time of our accident), moved into the house next to us a few months before our accident, and Tiffany and I hit it off immediately. We are so much alike it is scary. We take turns being there for each other. I encourage her with her parenting, she encourages me with my parenting, and we encourage each other on how to let go of the idea of perfection as mothers. We are both too hard on ourselves, want everyone else to be happy, and have a hard time saying no and accepting help from others. She was in her third trimester of pregnancy with her second child when she and Ava came over with activities in tow to hang out with Cailee.

I might not have been so willing to accept her help, but I thought it would actually do her some good as she tends to overdo it. I thought hanging out with Cailee would force her to sit and have some down time with the girls. Ava was so cute; she realized things were not quite right with Cailee, so she would bring things to her and "help" her. Cailee adores Ava, so she was thrilled to have them come over. We had many other offers from people to stay with Cailee, but unless Cailee knew them well, it was not something she was comfortable with. Gail was the only other person she jumped at the chance to hang out with. My plan was to make sure I got Cailee to the bathroom before I left, so Tiffany did not have to lift her.

Cailee, in her pink body cast, and Ava hanging out at home after the accident.

The first day of school took a lot to pull off. Our niece, Alison, was attending college in Madison that year, and she and her mother, Chrissy, stayed with us the day before school started. It was nice to have the extra help getting everyone off to school that day. With forms, lunches, coordinating all of the schedules, gym shoes (although Natania and Cailee would not be needing them for a while), backpacks, and changes of clothes, we had to make sure nothing fell through the cracks. I was glad I ordered the girls' school supplies through the school fundraiser earlier in the summer. Most of their school shopping had been done before the accident, and anything they didn't have was put off for some time.

Walking into school that day created quite a commotion. Between the children gathering around the girls—some asking what happened, others knowing what happened, and giving hugs and inquiring how they were doing—and the parents and teachers asking me all about it, I think many people ran late for prayers that morning. I'll never forget how Kianna's third grade teacher from the previous year, Mrs. Austin, said she cried when she heard about our accident and all of our sweet little girls. She and Kianna got along so well, and she was special to us. She always took the time to talk to the girls and thought Kianna was such a helpful, good big sister.

Once we got in the door and through morning prayers, I talked to the teachers about the girls' restrictions. I did not want to create such attention and emotion, but it was hard not to. Kianna was fine getting herself to class, but the twins and Cailee were not ready to leave my side. I pushed Cailee around in the twins' classroom to talk to their teacher, and then I attempted to get back to Cailee's class to get her situated. Once I finally convinced Natania and Brialle they would be OK in their new kindergarten class and that I'd check on them soon, I got Cailee into her K4 class. The children in her class did not know what to think about Cailee's body cast. They seemed afraid to talk to her because she was different. This concept was new to most four-year-olds. She had no control over where she was going, because she needed me to push her. Although she had the wheelchair available so she could learn to get around herself a bit, she opted for her old umbrella stroller. Unfortunately, that choice limited her attempts at independence.

After the initial "stir," it was free-play time. I took her over to the chalkboard so she could draw while I tried to get the forms handed in to her teacher. About the same time the principal, Sister Kathleen, came in to see how we were doing.

As I was talking to her about how we were all faring, I heard Cailee crying. She was surrounded by kids, sitting in the middle of all of them, feeling very overwhelmed. A couple of the boys started hitting or banging on her pink body cast on the chest and leg, laughing at how hard it was. I quickly explained that they could not hit at it, that it hurt her. I felt bad that Cailee felt so out of control with the situation. She clung to me and cried, pleading with me not to leave her alone again.

It's important to try to see the positive in situations. In this light, I have to say it was quite fun to attend school with Cailee. Her teacher had her hands full with thirteen children, nine of which were boys. I was not great help initially, because I had to sit down often. I was still recuperating myself. But I quickly realized that my being there was a good thing. The teacher needed an extra hand, and I could offer that. Although Cailee's classes were 8–11a.m. every day, we only came every other day. With all the doctors' appointments and scheduling conflicts, I could not do it every day. I felt bad about the days we were not there. There were certain things the teacher could not do in the classroom without another adult present.

Cailee's healing process was a learning experience for us. Since they did not surgically align her leg with the steel rod, and instead "set" it back together and casted her, there was a chance her broken bone would shift. An x-ray showed it had shifted significantly. By this time, Dr. Noonan was able to see her as a clinic patient. We were grateful that he was caring for Cailee and felt she was in good hands, but we were upset by the significant shift shown on her x-ray. There were two possibilities as to what we would do from there. First, they could try to "wedge" the cast to attempt to shift her bone a bit closer. If it could be shifted within 30 degrees, it would be OK. If the wedging was not successful, she would have to go into the hospital again to be re-casted, with her under anesthesia again. We were crossing our fingers. When we went back again, it showed that her leg had shifted back within reasonable measures. Although it still showed the bones next to each other, rather than connecting where it broke, Dr. Noonan said it would eventually create a "ball" of bone around the break. Then, over time, it would stretch out and heal as she grew. If it wasn't for our trust in Dr. Noonan, we may have thought he was crazy. The human body is amazing.

We also learned that it can actually be better for the child when the leg heals like this. When the bone breaks, it grows more bone as it heals to compensate for the break. When this happens, it can make the bone longer than if the break had never happened. If this were the case, Cailee's leg would have been longer than the other. In her case, the way it was healing, her leg was temporarily shorter but would even out in time. I know, sounds strange, doesn't it?

When it came time for Cailee to get her cast off, it was exciting but nerve-wracking. She was concerned when it came time for them to saw it off. If you've ever had a cast and had this done, you know what I mean. You close your eyes and hope like heck they don't cut too deep. It took awhile, but they sawed, pried it apart, and it eventually came off.

I did not anticipate how long it would take to ease Cailee back into life. She was afraid to be moved or touched, because she thought her leg would hurt. The skin that had been under her cast was very dry and scaly. I also anticipated atrophy of her leg, although I was delightfully surprised when it was not that bad.

When we got her home, my first plan was to get her into the bathtub. Since her body cast was at an angle—to the point that she was sort of leaning back all the time, her back muscles were weak. Because of this, she was unable to sit in the bathtub without holding herself up with her arms behind her as she did for so long when she had her cast on. Every time I touched her, she whimpered. I had little luck trying to "exfoliate" the dead skin, but I was able to gently wash her from head to toe for the first time in a long time.

Getting her dressed after her bath was also a challenge. Again she whimpered when the clothes I put on her touched her skin. She did not want to move her legs at all. In the tub, I encouraged her to wiggle her toes or bend her knees to get used to the idea. It got better over time. It took a good week before she attempted to put any weight on her leg.

I remember one time she was holding onto the trunk in the family room. She was feeling quite confident, trying to hobble/hop around it, when suddenly she lost her balance and fell backward. We were very nervous that she might have done some damage to her leg, since she was still fragile. Her leg was OK, but it did set her back a bit with her confidence.

Meanwhile, we tried to keep Natania calm to prevent her from bumping her arm. Not having a cast was challenging, as she had no protection. I was nervous about the kids at school. Each day she came home and told me how one of the kids accidentally bumped her arm. I was so proud of her though; she was enjoying kindergarten, and although she missed me when she was at school, she did plow on.

Brialle did great with her healing. She ended up with a black eye, as did I. In fact, we matched; we both had black eyes on our left eyes. We continued to apply antibiotic ointment three times a day and to take oral antibiotics to prevent our chances of infection, but our lacerations were healing well. Our plastic surgeon from UW Hospital, Dr. Bentz, was wonderful. Brialle absolutely loved him. He was sweet and attentive to her. He also worked with adults, so we were lucky to see him at the same time. We were there quite often at first. We had our initial appointment with him to ensure our injuries were not getting infected and to check how our stitches were doing. After a few days, we were both able to get the stitches out from around our eyes. I went first so I could tell Brialle what to expect. It hurt, but it was nothing like it was when they went in. When Brialle got her stitches out, she was a trooper. They said she was the best patient.

I had to go back a few days later so the stitches on my legs could be taken out. That was different; there were over 150 of them, so it took a long time. Several were embedded into my skin, which made it harder. Tim was there to hold my hand. I was grateful to have my stitches out. It had been difficult to remove my dressings with the stitches in. I learned how valuable medicated, non-stick dressings were. They were expensive, but worth every penny. Without them, the bandages stuck to my stitches. As I removed the dressing, it pulled at the stitches, as well as any newly developed healing (scabbing). The non-stick dressings were applied on top of the ointment before the bandages that wrapped around my legs. On top of that, I had to wrap ace bandages around my legs to keep the bandages on. I said good-bye to jeans for a while and wore skirts for some time. Cailee was not the only one who looked dressed up all the time.

Brialle was happy to have her stitches out. The puncture laceration under her brow was our greatest concern. As it healed, it formed a lump that made the doctor wonder if it was just scar tissue or possibly some glass still embedded under the skin. Tim and I shared that the plastic surgeon that took care of her in Green Bay was able to get it out. When the doctor heard this, he assumed it was just significant scar tissue. Over time, he said it would lessen.

We were healing physically, but healing mentally and emotionally was another story. The girls were up every night, either from nightmares or wanting to be with one of us. Natania did not want me out of her sight. Since she was with me when I fainted in the emergency room (we later learned that she thought I had died when I collapsed), she momentarily experienced the tough reality of what it was like to lose her mother. She would tell me over and over again how much she loved me and, "You're the best Mommy in the entire world."

She told Tim the same thing: "You're the best Daddy in the entire world."

Our nights were not restful for several months. Cailee cried out in her sleep, screaming or whimpering, and calling out for me on a nightly basis. She wanted me to be with her until she fell asleep. In the beginning, I was unable to lie down with her because of my legs. To make it easier for me, Tim brought the rocking chair next to her bed for me to sit on. She would be OK with me holding her hand and just being with her. The only problem was when I tried to get up after she fell asleep, she'd sense it and want me to stay. Then Natania would be up and also wanted me to sit by her so she could fall back to sleep. As in the old days, if they were both awake at the same time, it was a challenge. Then Tim would get up with one. Kianna and Brialle slept OK most of the time, despite the occasional nightmares.

Kianna felt guilty that everyone was hurt except her. I told her how happy we were that she was OK and that God knew she would be a tremendous helper with everyone. And she was. As a thank-you, we bought her a special "Candy Bouquet" to acknowledge all she did for us. With all of the attention her sisters got, she deserved this special gift.

Driving continues to be a problem. As I type this part of the chapter, we are traveling back from an RV trip to Yellowstone. We thought it would be fun to rent an RV. It's been great, but I am almost crazy with worry. Every time we take a turn I feel like we are going to flip over. Each winding road in the mountains has tremendous cliffs—right out the RV window—and makes me feel like I'm going to lose it.

I've been doing a lot of praying this trip. In my book I write about trusting God, but that does not mean I don't still struggle with things. Since our accident, I constantly worry about getting into another accident. I realize how many nut cases are out on the road, drinking and driving, being aggressive, or just not paying attention. I also learned that we are not in control of our lives. Life is precious, and it takes only a moment to change your life. I also realize how blessed we all were. I'm so grateful we are all alive and no one is paralyzed or disfigured or in chronic pain. The whole experience has been a valuable lesson, has brought me closer to God, and is probably the event that finally pushed me to finish this book. Yes, it was a valuable lesson.

CHAPTER 19

ALL COMING
FULL CIRCLE

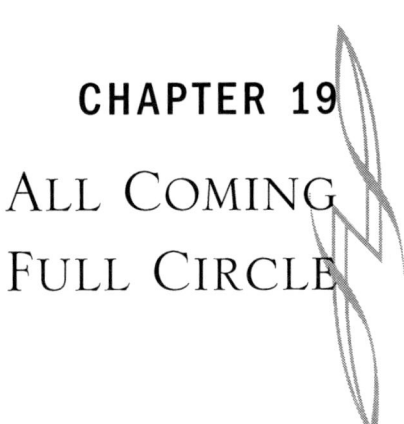

I WAS HOPING OUR lives would calm down for once, but shortly after our accident, I began to suspect that some old issues with my endometriosis were on the comeback. The familiar stabbing pains that came out of nowhere and the achiness that came from my remaining ovary made me realize I needed to try to preempt any serious problems.

An appointment with my doctor confirmed I did indeed have an ovarian cyst. I remember back when I was taking the fertility drugs and Lupron, I was concerned about what I was doing to my body long term. Researchers did not know what the long-term ramifications were of the drugs, and after further research, I learned I was at high risk for ovarian cancer.

I knew in my heart I would be OK, and that God was going to ensure that I was listening carefully to my body, yet newer research continued to show a link to endometriosis and cancer. The use of the menopausal drug and cancer were also connected. When I combined this knowledge with the knowledge that fertility drugs can also cause ovarian cancer, I was eager to take care of things quickly.

After Cailee was born, I experienced periods that were sporadic and lasted quite long. I also found myself to be on an emotional roller coaster. My doctor joked with me that anyone who was not getting sleep at night and had such long periods would be irritable. We decided to start me on a low-level hormone pill to help even things out. The pill would also help "ward off" my endometriosis and buy me some time in this area.

It helped for a couple of years, but when women hit thirty-five, they need to start considering the negative effects of the pill. Women who have families with a history of heart disease are not encouraged to take the pill. I had experienced some peculiar heart-related events a couple of times—sharp pain in my chest and shortness of breath, which was considered in the decision. After further checking, they suspected I might have a slight heart valve issue that only came up one or two times a year. The shortness of breath might be anxiety/panic or asthma related. The episodes were so far apart that I did not worry about it, but they also did a "C-reactive protein" test that tests your blood for possible future heart disease. Mine was seven times the normal level. All of this led us to the decision to stop taking the pill.

A year later my problems started occurring again. My doctor was not surprised. She said it is typically a year or so before these issues start to take over. We made the decision to have a total hysterectomy; this meant they would take out my uterus and remaining ovary. As I'm writing this, I am still recovering.

On June 9, 2006, I said good-bye to my (abdominal) female organs. I had mixed emotions, but mostly I was grateful that my uterus, which caused me so many issues in my life, also gave me four incredible children. I was overwhelmed with happiness that this was happening now instead of when I was twenty-six and without children. A hysterectomy back then would have devastated me.

In preparing for my surgery, a woman from Pastoral Care visited me. Without going into a lot of detail, I shared with her what was going on. At one point I became so emotional and was crying so hard that I could not talk. The poor dear was concerned, thinking I was having a hard time accepting the procedure. When I finally composed myself, however, she was relieved when I told her the real reason I was crying. I shared with her that I was just so overjoyed to have four amazing children and how grateful I was that I was having the surgery now rather than earlier.

With four children, the planning and logistics of the surgery was important. I could take care of myself perhaps, but there was no way I could keep up with the demands of motherhood while I recuperated. My surgery was on a Friday, and I got out of the hospital on a Sunday. During this time, my parents took my three younger children to their hobby farm, while Tim and Kianna stuck around, visiting me in the hospital and attending soccer activities.

My parents then came back and helped out a few more days, and then my in-laws came to take over.

I am very blessed to have family willing and able to help us out. During this time I've often thought of people who are on their own and who are ill—the elderly who are struggling and those going through cancer treatments. Even small things like grocery shopping are a challenge. For me, I could not drive for two weeks. Not only is my family around, but also we have wonderful friends who have delivered meals made with love. Our neighbor, Mary, took the time to ask me what we needed from the grocery store so she could drop it off for me. If everyone took responsibility for family, neighbors, and friends, it would make such a difference in the world. So much wonderful help is given to so many, yet I think about those who are forgotten.

The surgery went well. My doctor really didn't know what to expect with my history and was pleasantly surprised by what she found. She was concerned she'd find a mess with endometriosis, but not only did she find minimal to no endometriosis in my abdominal cavity, she also confirmed everything was benign. Tests revealed that I had some endometriosis growing through my uterine wall, however. Knowing this confirmed that the decision was the right one.

I have experienced some sadness regarding the hysterectomy. Although I was not planning to have more children, it is difficult to think of the finality of the procedure. When I see mothers with their young babies, or expectant mothers, I feel in a strange sort of way that I'm not part of the "club" anymore. I'm now different from them, and that chapter of my life is closed. Permanently. I realize, again, however, just how grateful I am for my incredible children.

I am happy about the stage my children are at. They are growing quickly and have developed such wonderful yet different personalities. It's actually getting easier and, mostly because they are finally (almost) sleeping through the nights, I am becoming "normal" again.

It is funny when I think back to when they were all toddlers. I realize how I seldom looked "up." It's crazy, but I was always doing what I called the "chicken-head cocking." I was constantly watching my children and trying to ensure their safety at all times. Now that they are older and can play on their play set without constant fear of injury, I can finally take a deep breath once in a while and admire them. I can also look up at the beautiful sky once in a while.

In addition to this, I am able to reflect on the last fifteen years of my life and take time to fulfill my promise to God—to witness to others about what God has done for me in my life once I learned how to trust and listen.

This brings me "full circle"—hence the name of this book.

And as I come "full circle," I will try to tie up any loose ends. Whenever I read books, I like the feeling of closure.

Overall, we are doing fine. It's been almost a year since our accident, and Cailee is doing well. In fact, Cailee is one of the superstars on her soccer team. At only five years old, she hopes to fill her big sister Kianna's shoes some day. Kianna is part of a competitive soccer league and it's Cailee's goal to join them some day as well. Watching her at one of her recent soccer games, she scored five goals. I heard positive comments from many parents, and I was proud to hear the coach on the opposing team ask me, "Is she *your* daughter? Wow, she is really good!" They don't know the half of it. It brings tears to my eyes to watch her fly down the field super fast as she scores a goal. She's come a long way since her pink body-cast days.

Natania is doing well. She and Brialle will be seven in October 2006. She is still tiny—only weighs

34 lbs.—and has yet to get on the weight charts, but her height is fine, and she will be the first to tell you she's the smartest of the family. She's reading now, as is Brialle. It melts my heart to watch them try to teach their "baby sister" how to read too.

Natania continues to have some slight physical complaints. She often experiences pain in her feet at night, and wakes me to massage her feet. She also has some pain around her belly button area. We consulted with a specialist on this. Oddly enough, he said she was complaining of her umbilical vein that was palpable on a physical examination. He said he has not heard they can hurt, although he's never been able to feel one on somebody before either. It is likely due to her slender size. As her mom, I think if she is particularly active, which she often is, it can become strained. But what do I know?

Unfortunately, there is not a lot we can do to help except offer Tylenol for comfort. We still worry about her weight, mostly because she gets knocked over easily, but that does not stop her from playing soccer and playing chase with anyone who is interested. When she plays soccer, I try hard not to be overprotective. However, at her soccer game two nights ago, I was ready to punch a little girl (not really, I'm just making a point again) who slammed into Natania's chest. She does experience pain around her sternum/chest area from time to time. My theory is since her ribs were put back together with "chicken wire" after her open-heart surgery, she experiences pain as she is growing. I feel we have to be careful when rough housing with her so we don't hurt her chest. With her soccer, I am grateful that Daddy is their coach so he can keep an eye out for her.

As far as Natania's heart goes, aside from periodic checkups with Dr. Weinhaus, we keep an eye out for infection and illness. If she is exposed to certain infections, it could go to her heart. For this reason, she needs to receive an antibiotic before she goes to the dentist or if she has an infected wound. We try not to dwell on any of this. In the back of my mind, I find myself worrying, but if/when I do, I say a prayer that God will help Natania, and that if anything is a concern, to help us identify it in time to get her the help she needs.

The greatest achievement in my mind for Natania is that she learned to ride her bike without training wheels! I was concerned about her ever learning, because she is so small and top heavy (her head is normal size). She does not have the greatest balance. But as afraid as I was, I tried to cover up my concern and encourage her every step of the way. I had to really trust Tim to run alongside of her and ensure that she would not get hurt. He did not let us down.

She was nervous every time she tried to ride her bike. She'd say, "Mom, can you say a prayer for me and wish me luck?" When she went from Tiffany's driveway to Mary's without help from Daddy or falling, I was overjoyed. As I hugged her, tears fell from my eyes. I was and am so grateful for how far she has come.

Kianna will be eleven soon and is remarkably bright. She's still as strong and beautiful as ever. She continues to be very protective of her little sisters and takes the role seriously. She is looking forward to babysitting them in the next year or two. As I mentioned above, Kianna is strong in soccer and is very athletically inclined— something she definitely does *not* get from me.

Brialle is eager to please and reminds me most of myself when I was young. She is empathetic and easy going. While she has done well with soccer, she has a lot of interest in doing ballet this year. This too is more like me, as dance was my passion. As far as the effects of the accident, her scars will always be there, but they are not very noticeable, unless someone looks closely.

We have many wonderful friends and family to be thankful for as well as new friends and godchildren we love. My friend Gail and her husband, Dan, after they experienced their own challenges in having a child, have a beautiful little boy named Noah. He looks like his dad but has his mother's bold strength and ambition. We get together with them often, and the girls love watching and "mothering" baby Noah.

The girls also have a god-sister, Chelsea, and their first new god-brother, named Noah as well. They are the beautiful children of my dear cousin Iileen and her husband, David. We all love their visits.

If you recall, my neighbor Tiffany was very pregnant when she and her daughter, Ava, helped us out with Cailee after our accident. Tiffany had her second baby, and they named him Zachary. He has a wonderful, big smile and we all enjoy spending time with Tiffany, Ava, and Zach. We couldn't ask for better neighbors.

In closing *Full Circle*, I'd like to reflect on what I've learned during my "circle." As I mentioned in my preface, God doesn't promise every day will be a day without challenges, but if you seek him, God is there to help you through them. While God gives us free will, he does want us to trust in him and ask for his guidance in our lives. We are not in control of our lives. Every time we try to control, God reminds us that *he* is in charge. Having the ability to trust in God also helped me to understand what it means to truly be content and be filled with peace.

Once I finally learned that I do not have to worry, control, or fear (and through a *lot* of patience and prayer), God blessed us with Kianna. When I stopped trying to control the process and let him do it his way, he gave us Brialle and Natania. He taught us that we couldn't fix Natania's heart. We learned what it was to be truly vulnerable as he took the worry away and guided the doctors with skill and care. He blessed us with Cailee to prove that he gave me all of the "tools" to have children if I would just let it happen on *his* timeline. He took care of Otis when I (and his adoptive family) asked for his help. And just in case our belief was waning, he protected us through our car accident and taught us that life is short, life is precious, and yes, indeed, God is in charge.

I believe God's hand was in my surgery as a way to help me maintain a healthy body to care for my children and to ensure my ability to share my story of God's blessings.

We all have choices in our lives. Some may wonder if some of the things I've discussed in my book were coincidences; some may wonder if I tried too hard to identify how things tied together; and others may wonder how I could see the positive in the midst of many challenges. There are people who look at the positive and count their blessings. I am one of those people. I see the silver lining in every dark cloud, and I appreciate each experience I have had in my life. I feel wiser and stronger, and most of all, at peace knowing that if I do trust in God, he will continue to lead me in my short time in this world.

I know there are many people who have gone through so much more, and to them, even in the midst of their pain and sorrow, I again remind you that you are not alone. God is always there.

Tomorrow, our family will pack up and head north to our cottage for the weekend. Like all other trips, in what has become our ritual since the accident, the kids will ask that we say a prayer as we get on the road. We will ask God to protect us as we travel, to help us be safe, protect us from harm, keep us out of any accidents, and help other drivers to be safe. You see, one of the greatest lessons our children learned from the accident, and one we could not have taught them on our own, was to trust God, accept that he is in control, and offer up our worries to him in prayer. And they do. What a blessing to have learned this so young.

After reading my book, I hope you have a greater understanding of what it is to have faith. It's always a learning process. Challenges will still happen, but you are never alone. Just open up your heart, be honest with God about everything—good and bad—and then trust him to lead you. It ties back to the "Tapestry" poem in the beginning of the book. When you trust, in the end, it all comes together, "Full Circle," and results in a beautiful story (or tapestry).

May God be with you.

CHAPTER 20

THE UNEXPECTED
CHAPTER

WELL, HERE I am. It's July 10, 2007, and the clock on my computer reads 11:06 p.m. I fully intended to have sent my proposal off to publishers long before this point. Life is interesting. From one year to the next (sometimes even one day to the next) you never know what life will bring.

As I hoped you've discovered by reading my book, I learned over the years to *try* to listen to God. After I finished (I thought) my manuscript, I felt God telling me to "sit tight." Honestly, I was a bit surprised by this, considering the fire I had in my belly to move forward in sharing my story. At the same time, I was becoming a bit overwhelmed with it all. The floodgates had opened, and everywhere I turned, I felt I had been given the ability to see into other people's souls. I was drawn like a magnet to people who seemed to need me. I felt like I couldn't even go to the grocery store or take the girls out for ice cream without a very heavy draw for me to approach a person who was reaching out for spiritual help.

During this time, I felt like God was helping me choose the right words to reach out to these people. I was on a roll.

For example, last October I was invited to speak at a Women's Ministry event through our church. Shortly before the event, Tim and I were going to a weekend retreat for his company in beautiful Minocqua, Wisconsin. The timing for writing my speech was perfect. The afternoon we arrived, my husband was scheduled to golf with a group of coworkers. I was excited to retreat to our room to write my speech. It was the first time in a very long time I had time *all* to myself in a quiet, peaceful setting. I prayed and asked God to help me write the words that would make the most significant difference to the people attending the event.

The words flowed. I practiced it, and it felt really good. What happened the next day amazed me. I was feeling particularly in touch with nature and the beauty of God's world. My heart was full, and every breath I took felt so clean and crisp. I felt more alive and fulfilled than I think I've ever felt in my life. I decided to take a book down to a long dock on the property and sit on a chair overlooking the beautiful lake. While I was reading and taking it all in, a woman came up to me and struck up a conversation. I had met her briefly that morning at breakfast, and she said there was something about me that made her feel she could talk to me. It turns out not only did she end up sharing difficulties she was facing with me, but also she was someone who was greatly guided by God.

I have no idea how, but we started talking about our faith. She had amazing stories about how God worked through her. The story that really got through to me was a time when God spoke to her and told her she was to give a gift of the crucifix to a man she barely knew, with whom she worked. She said God put it strongly upon her heart, but she was uncomfortable with the idea. She said she "fought" the idea. God continued to put it very strongly upon her heart, and she worried that the guy would think she was crazy. She didn't even know if he was a Christian.

Finally, she said to God, "OK, OK. *Fine*, I'll do it!" She was led to the man's home to give the cross to him. The guy was there, and when he opened the door, she blurted out, "I'm supposed to give this to you." She put the crucifix (or cross as I like to call it) in his hand. He broke down and cried and shared that he was terminally ill. He died two weeks later.

Isn't that amazing?

In October, I delivered my speech. I am an admittedly tough critic of myself, yet I felt my speech was one of the best I'd ever given. People asked me if I was nervous, and I said no because I was just a vehicle God used to connect with people. My story was because of God's guidance, and I was standing in front of all of these women for him. People came up to me afterward and told me how great I did and how much they were impacted by my story. I even received a delightful letter from someone stating how much I did for her. Many shared that I spoke to each person from my heart, rather than speaking *at* them. I only wanted to make a difference, but the attention on *me* was and always is difficult for me. Most people do not know this, since people might describe me as a "social butterfly." But the truth is, I am only out to make others comfortable, happy, and welcome. If I see someone who looks lonely, I take it upon myself to try to make them happy.

Things continued to happen in terms of connecting with people, although life with four children, my part-time job, and everything else started to overwhelm me. I openly cried to God and asked him for help. I was beginning to feel like I had to save the world and do so much—so much that it was creating an imbalance in our family life. I prayed openly and explained to God how I was feeling. I was in over my head.

Very soon after that, it was as if that "door" closed. Not quite all the way, but it closed enough to give me some breathing room. Part of me felt like a failure, but at the same time, I knew God was offering me a break from it all. I recently learned why I was to be put on hold for a while. The reason was I had another chapter to add to my book, although at the time I had no idea.

Now I'm going to move back to December 18, 2006. Tim, the girls, and I were going to my parent's home to celebrate Christmas with my mother's side of the family. My brother, Dean, was there too. When we got there, I was shocked to see the appearance of my brother. He didn't look well. He tried to smile and was sweet as usual and came to greet us. I said, "Dean, you don't look very well! Are you sick?" He said something like, "Yeah, I've had a cold." At the time I suspected perhaps he had a touch of the flu and suggested he be careful not to get too close to everyone so others wouldn't catch his bug. I felt bad for him because I knew how much he loved family gatherings and realized he must have felt pretty bad. Mom told me Dean had a doctor's appointment coming up that week and maybe he could shed some light.

Shortly after, I saw my brother on Christmas Eve at our home. It is tradition for us to have my immediate family over for Christmas Eve dinner. Tim and I prepare the meal with the help of the girls and we get out the fine China (the China my parents got for their wedding) and we eat in the dining room. This year was particularly fun, as we were able to use our new dining room set and hutch. We had gotten it just a couple of days before. It was our first "nice" furniture group, intended to be large enough to accommodate our Christmas Eve dinners and the ones that someday may include future son-in-laws. Yes, that sure is planning ahead!

I remember Dean walking through the door from our garage into our kitchen. I gasped when I saw him. He appeared puffy and had an unusual color to his face. I said, "Dean, you look terrible!" I know, not a very nice thing to say, but I was concerned.

Mom said he had *not* gone to the doctor, and she was very concerned—she thought it was possible that Dean had pneumonia. She said she would take him in on December 26 to see what was wrong.

Dean is usually so excited about family gatherings. Almost equally as exciting to him is a good meal. What made us feel particularly concerned about Dean was that we noticed he didn't eat much. Usually he'd gobble up the ham, potatoes, and everything else quicker than anyone. When we went to church that night, Dean was lethargic, although over the last year that behavior seemed to come and go. He was often medicated, including a prescription for depression. It was true he had not seemed his upbeat self during the last year, but most thought it was due to depression and frustration. He was having challenges in his job as well. In the last year, he seemed disinterested and was calling in sick more. We tried to get to the bottom of it.

Mom and Dad had repeatedly tried to talk to him over the last few months, and they learned he was feeling "rushed" and pressured to do his job faster. He's never been the type to like any kind of stress or conflict, so it made sense that he would do almost anything to avoid it. I also took him to lunch and asked him to share what was going on. He was doing a repetitive type of job every day. His options were limited. Sure, they would move him to a different job once in a while, but it was the same. If he was happy, then I was happy; but it upset me that he was unhappy now. As an adult, I could call in sick to work (except as a mom), and I had options. If I didn't like my job, I could do something about it, or find another job. In Dean's case, he didn't have a lot of options. It became a vicious cycle. He didn't want to go to work, so he'd call in sick or do something to get out of it. When he did this, he frustrated his employer and our parents.

When Dean was little, he never liked it when people around him yelled or fought. He was an easy victim to those who would tease or bully him into doing something he didn't think he should do. His plan was to avoid them. If I knew about it, I'd deal with it—anything to protect my brother.

Back to Christmas Eve. It no longer seemed like his behavior could be chalked up to depression. When we took his picture, he had a difficult time smiling. We had to prod him to smile—very unlike Dean. We did get one nice picture of him smiling as he held up a Badger v-neck golf top we bought for him. He loved anything

Badgers or Green Bay Packers. During all of this, I tried to talk with Dean to determine what might be wrong. I asked him if he had any idea what might be wrong and asked him a bunch of questions. He looked at me very seriously and said, "I wish I knew."

I gave him a hug good-bye that night and was anxious to hear from Mom what the doctor said after his appointment. Shortly afterwards, Mom told me the doctor suspected pneumonia, although Mom started suspecting that Dean was in congestive heart failure. Mom was a registered nurse, and I was always grateful that she was there to watch out for Dean. As soon as she said "congestive heart failure," it all made sense to me. I remembered when Natania was in the hospital and what the symptoms were. Mom said the doctor wanted to first rule out pneumonia before looking deeper. We were all concerned that the doctor was putting off something that may have been very serious. After a couple of days, Dean went in again.

Between Christmas and New Year's, Tim and I were planning our fifth Annual "Natania's Night," where we raise money for the hospitals that helped her. It was our way of giving back to the hospitals so they could help families offset the costs of having a baby in long-term, intensive care. This party was extra special, as we had a guest of honor joining us this year—Jennifer. It was wonderful to have Jennifer in town. She helped us prepare for the party any way we needed her. She even helped clean the house.

On a side note: Remember the dream Jennifer had when we first discovered I was pregnant with the twins, about two children walking on the beach? She saw a framed photo we took of the twins walking on the beach in Mexico a couple of years ago. They were holding hands. Tim took the picture while the girls were out walking with him early one morning. I never thought anything about it.

When Jen saw the picture, she was in the middle of talking to me about something. She stopped and said, "Oh my God, Diane!" I thought, *Oh my gosh, what is it?* She practically gave me a heart attack. She said, "That photo! That was my dream! Is that the twins? Oh my God! That is the vision I had all those years ago when you were pregnant with them! Remember?" I had forgotten all about that dream, honestly. I vaguely remembered it, and then it came back to me. I remembered when she told me the dream, I was happy she saw two children, although I remember how hearing about the size difference of the two did not settle with me very well. It was amazing that after all this time the girls had gone through a lot and had come a long way.

Her presence was a blessing more than I realized. The day of the party, Mom called to tell me Dean had been admitted to the hospital. They believed he had what was called "cardiac myopathy," a.k.a. a weak heart, in addition to congestive heart failure.

From that point on, I was a mess. Jennifer helped ground me. Having her there to comfort me meant more to me than she could ever know. Although we decided to go ahead with the party, I was having a hard time focusing and felt very scatter-brained as we greeted and talked with our friends. The night turned out to be special, as usual. We were surrounded by so many people we hold near and dear to our hearts. I knew I didn't have to explain myself. Most heard throughout the night about my brother's condition and offered to pray for him.

The next day, I was anxious to get to the hospital to see Dean. Tim and I stopped at the gift shop to pick up a card, a magazine, and a crossword puzzle book. He was staying at Fort Atkinson Hospital, and the people seemed nice. The facility was new. Dean had a large, comfortable room. When I first saw him, he seemed more like himself in terms of behavior. Oh, what a blessing that was! He was still quite puffy. It was particularly obvious because I could see his ankles (he was wearing one of those attractive "gowns"). One of the first symptoms of congestive heart failure is swollen ankles. The doctor's first priority was to reduce some of the stress on his heart by administering a diuretic to reduce the water retention in his body and around his heart. He was carrying around a lot of extra weight for this reason. No wonder he felt bad.

When we walked in, he looked at us. I could tell he was scared but happy to see us. He reminded me of a little boy in a man's body. We talked about many things—what the doctors said, how he was feeling, how we were happy to know what was going on. He also mentioned it was scary. We talked a little bit about the worst-case scenario—we are all going to end up in the same place someday, in heaven. We talked about how heaven is a wonderful place and there is no fear or pain there. I cannot remember everything we talked about, but I was grateful he was more "in the moment" and able to carry on a nice conversation, particularly one that could offer the depth that was needed.

When we left, I gave him another big hug and told him I loved him. I felt bad that he needed to go through all of this.

I called Dean a couple of times while he was in the hospital. He was losing weight every day—maybe even too fast. He was finally discharged from the hospital and stayed with Mom and Dad to recuperate.

My parents were trying to decide how best to continue his care—in Madison or in Fort Atkinson. We had gotten some names of cardiologists at St. Mary's/ Dean Care and felt it might be best to continue with them. Mom knew of a great doctor who had cared for a good friend of hers. Unfortunately, he was not available for an immediate appointment, but another doctor was recommended. An appointment was made within a week of Dean's hospital stay. I made arrangements so I could attend the doctor's appointment with them.

While I've always been satisfied with my parents taking care of everything, this was the first time anything significant had happened in our family, and I wanted to be there. I wanted to be present to support my brother and Mom and Dad. The doctor was difficult to read. I think he was trying hard not to alarm us, but he knew how grave Dean's situation was. He was very serious when he said Dean had a very weak heart. We were all confused and very concerned. At that point, Dean was still bloated, and we could tell he was preoccupied (for good reason). We had no idea what to expect. Dean was wondering why I was there for the appointment, Mom later shared with me. He thought it meant it was really bad. Mom told him I was there because the girls were all in school and it was in Madison. As we were walking out of the doctor's office, Dean was really struggling. He couldn't walk very far without having a hard time breathing, and he had to sit down. Finally, we found a wheelchair for him. He was stoic and strong but scared.

He was soon scheduled for a cardiac catheterization to help the doctors take a closer look at his heart. This is when they go up through the groin into an artery to go up into his heart and determine if there are any blockages. They didn't find any. This was interesting, because when you hear of people with heart disease, it is typically due to high cholesterol and not eating healthy that results in blockages. It made us wonder what caused the cardiomyopathy. They said it could have been from a virus or possibly the result of a congenital issue never diagnosed. They really did not know. We believe it was most likely a virus that got into his heart.

He went through the procedure with flying colors. He was such a sweetheart and didn't complain once. He loved the attention of the nurses and was always polite to them. When I visited him, we went on and on about how brave he was. He wasn't supposed to move very much, and when he got his food (still bland due to his special low fluid, low sodium diet), he kept moving his head up to eat. I offered to feed him and made jokes about how his little sister would take care of it. I was spoon-feeding his Jell-O to him, and Mom and Dad took a picture. It was a special memory for me. If I could have fed him doses of love and healing, I would have. I forgot about this memory until just now, when I am forced to remember the details. It brings tears to my eyes.

Dean seemed to be doing well. He was feeling better every day as he continued to lose water weight. The doctor increased his Lasix dosage, and he lost a lot of weight.

He was discharged from the hospital, but soon after, he was back in the Emergency Room. This time they brought him to St. Mary's in Madison. Tim and

I were with the girls at the Olive Garden for dinner Friday night. It was after Kianna's soccer game. My cell phone rang, and I was concerned to see the number on the caller ID: it was Mom. She shared how Dean was back in the hospital due to significant rectal bleeding. She said he was feeling great, but they had to determine what was going on.

Later that same night, Natania was complaining a lot about her neck—she said it hurt "really bad." All through dinner she complained. She was in tears by the time we got home. I started to get a little nervous, because upon further investigation, I learned she also had a headache. Just to be safe, I called the doctor. She wanted to rule out meningitis—just in case.

Next thing I knew we were headed to St. Mary's Hospital. I called Mom and Dad to let them know. When we got there, the nurses let us see Dean while we waited for the doctor. I teased Dean about how crummy it was that he was back in the hospital but that soon he would be feeling better. In fact, he had been feeling so much better—he was looking forward to getting back to his own apartment again.

They ended up admitting Dean into the hospital for further observation. Natania ended up being fine. They suspected she simply pulled a muscle in her neck. They also did a quick strep test, and it turned out to be negative.

Dean was scheduled for a colonoscopy/gastroscopy to determine the source of his internal bleeding. He was on a strict fluid diet for his congestive heart failure, and there was some concern about the amount of fluid he'd have to drink to prepare for the colonoscopy. Mom was trying to work with the nurses to be sure the doctors worked together to determine where they went from there.

I went back to the hospital to see Dean as he was doing the "prep" for his procedure. He looked pretty bored by it all; he was just so anxious to get back to his life. Again, he didn't complain; he was a trooper. It was soon time for me to go, and I tried to give him a quick hug in the middle of all of his prep. If it were me going through this kind of prep, I wouldn't have wanted an audience, so I thought it would be best if we gave him some space. As I called out to say good-bye, he gave me a "thumbs-up," and I told him to hang in there.

The doctors found he had two ulcers. One was a newer one, and one was old. They treated him, and soon he was discharged.

Through all of this, he lost about fifty pounds. He looked very different. He said he felt great. He wanted to get back to his apartment again. He was forty-two years old and was tired of being told what to do all of the time.

Mom and Dad worked with Dean and the doctors to come up with a plan for Dean to remain independent.

Managing his care was a full-time job. He had to stay on a strict diet, weigh himself often, take his medications at the appropriate times, get himself to Cardiac Rehab, and ease back into his job again.

When I called Dean, we would joke around about how it was time for us to "take care of ourselves" and do what the doctor says in eating healthy and exercising. I told him it was my goal for the new year, too, and we should compare notes to see how each other did. He appeared to be doing well. I was proud of him and how he seemed to be taking everything seriously. Shortly after all of this, Dean began complaining of a sore back. It was difficult to determine exactly what was going on, although since he was not one to complain, Mom brought it up to the doctors. It was thought that he strained his back. He took Advil to help reduce pain and inflammation. It didn't appear to be an immediate concern.

In the midst of all of this, Tim and I were planning to take the girls on a trip to Mexico. It had been planned for a long time, and the week preceding the trip, I hadn't spoken to Dean. We were planning to get on an airplane early Monday morning, February 19.

Sunday night, just after dinnertime, I got a call from Mom that changed everything.

Dean had been at the circus that day with my Aunt Claire. It was a special day for both of them, as our Uncle Mike, Claire's husband, had passed away since the last time they attended the circus together. It was a last-minute decision on Claire's part. She was not sure if it would be too difficult for her; but in the end, she decided it was what Mike would have wanted.

In addition to the circus, they also stopped at a train show and ran into our cousin Iileen, her husband, David, and their children, Chelsie and Noah. That evening, Mom and Dad invited Dean and Claire for chicken dinner.

During dinner, it came out that Dean had not been managing his care as well as he originally made it sound. It was becoming increasingly difficult for him to maintain the continuous responsibilities in caring for himself—from preparing strict meals to taking his medications, checking his blood sugars, making careful notes, etc. It is hard for anyone to do all of this. Mom and Dad were trying to get him to be honest with them about how well he was handling everything. They were frustrated and worried. He didn't want to disappoint them, yet he was afraid to tell them the truth, because he knew they'd want to move him back home.

Suddenly Dean said, "I feel like I hurt on the inside." They asked, "Do you mean you feel sad because you feel we are upset with you? What can we do to help?"

Then all at once he slumped over, and he was gone.

God gently swooped down and scooped him up and . . . brought him home.

The ambulance came to my parent's home. Mom, Dad, and Claire had been working on him until they got there. It appeared as though he took one more breath at one point, but he was unable to be revived.

When Mom called me, the attendants were just getting ready to load him in the ambulance. Not knowing what was happening at the time, I answered the phone playfully, saying, "Were your ears burning? I was just about to call you!" She said, "Diane, I have to be serious. It's Dean; he's had a heart attack." I immediately headed into the pantry of the kitchen, away from the kids. I said, "Oh my God!" Tim came over immediately. Mom said they were working on him, but it didn't look good. I know Mom well enough to know she was trying to spare me the finality. I said, "Mom, tell me. Is he . . .?" She said, "I think so, honey." I just slumped to the floor in complete shock and tears. Tim held me as I sobbed on his shoulder. The girls kept asking what was wrong. I don't remember the details, but Tim eventually took the girls upstairs to talk to them while I took some time to get myself together.

The girls were praying for Dean not to have to suffer. They were praying for God to do what he felt was right for Dean. They were praying for Mom, Dad, and me. I was concerned for them too. Their uncle Dean may be gone. My brother—my dear, sweet brother—was experiencing something he had only recently been worrying about.

I had to get to the hospital as quickly as I could. As usual, when I'm in the middle of a major crisis, I called Jennifer from my (hands free) cell phone. Again she was my lifeline. Jen and I talked, and she kept me focused so I could drive. She always knows what to say. We talked about how Dean deserved nothing but the best. We talked about how lovingly God took Dean home. Dean did not suffer, and he died in the arms of my parents after a full, happy day.

We talked about how it was getting too difficult for Dean to care for himself and yet how he would have been miserable at Mom and Dad's. We talked about my guilt for not having been more adamant about him staying with me. After further discussion, I realized he would have been miserable at my home too. Our house is too loud for him (loud noises always bothered him). We talked about how now Dean could be our guardian angel. I also told her I strongly felt that there was a reason for the timing, even as it related to my family. There was a reason we were not to go to Mexico early the next morning.

I cannot describe how I was feeling when I walked into the hospital that night. Everything was so matter of fact. Dad was looking for me and let me into the room where Dean's body lay. I gave Dad a hug and wanted to do the same for my mother, but she was on the phone. She had been on the phone with people regarding the donation of his organs/tissues and with the coroner. It didn't seem to fit; it bothered me that I could not go over to Mom and hug her. Dad led me to Dean, and it was surreal.

Every time I've seen someone close to me who has died, it never really sinks in. It does not make any sense. Their body is only a shell.

Dean was lying on the table with a breathing tube down his throat. I think his eyes were a little open. He was so cold. His stubby little toes and feet were sticking out from the blanket. It looked like his body had been through a lot when they were trying to revive him. His hair was sticking up all over. The monitor's leads adhered to his chest were still on, and his head was back, in an awkward position. I held his cold hand and quietly prayed to him and God, as I knew now he was watching over us too. His hand was so lifeless and kind of stiff. I ran my fingers through his beautiful hair. We always complimented Dean on his thick head of full, dark hair. It now had some gray in it, but it was still full and beautiful. He had handsome features—gorgeous blue eyes, a tan complexion, and great hair. He was a nice mix of my parents and took after our father in everything, although he got his great hair from our mother. I always thought he was so handsome, despite his challenges. If he'd been 100%, he would have been a heart-breaker. As it was, he was popular with the ladies from Opportunities, the place he worked. He always had a girlfriend, and I had the pleasure of getting to know all but the most recent one.

When Mom finally got off the phone, we hugged and cried. Just the three of us. Our family was made up of a family of four: Mom, Dad, Son, and Daughter. Now it was just the three of us. There was a big void and will always be.

We were there for a while, talking about the sudden shock of it all and what happened. We also discussed plans to donate Dean's organs or tissues as well as schedule an autopsy to understand exactly what happened.

What we did not know until later was that an autopsy and organ donation cannot both happen due to the possibility of contamination. This was discouraging and did not make sense to me. Personally, I would have thought we could have asked them not to disturb the heart/lung area during the removal of organs and tissues, although this was not the case. We had to make a decision: do the autopsy but take away the chance for Dean to help others, or donate his tissues and organs, never knowing what had really caused his death. Mom asked me what I thought.

Typically I let her make these kinds of decisions, but as his sister, I did have some say. I felt bad for my mother because I knew how much she wanted answers, but the answers would not change the outcome. I told her it might help *me* from a health awareness perspective, but I already knew the likely fate of my future someday. We have a family history of heart attacks on both sides of our family, and I know what I should be doing to increase my longevity. My suggestion was to go ahead with the organ and tissue donation, as Dean always liked to help others and this was another way to do this, even after his death. *Note: Just before my book went to print, my parents received a letter from RTI Donor Services stating how he helped 33 people worldwide by being a donor.*

In the midst of all of this, a nurse came in to put ice packs over Dean's eyes. Their goal was to help preserve what they could for the purpose of donating.

I don't remember driving back home that night.

The next morning, instead of getting on an airplane to Mexico, I was back in the car to meet my parents at the funeral home. I did not want my parents to go through all of this alone. We picked out the songs, the prayers, and everything else we needed to plan. I also asked to write the obituary. I needed to honor Dean's life somehow. It was important to me to get across who Dean was.

It was still such a shock, but as I suspected, there was a reason for the timing of Dean's death. I knew how much Dean loved the family, me, and my girls, his nieces. I know he would have stepped up to help them if they ever needed him. It is hard to explain, but I felt like I knew his soul and knew of the sacrifice he would make for any one of us.

Monday morning, Natania woke up feeling ill and vomiting. Tim was going to stay home with the girls while I was with my parents. He would keep me informed of how she was doing. She had vomited a few more times, and we kept thinking how difficult it would have been if she were on the airplane during all of this. While it may not have been life threatening (although it can become serious for Natania if we are not careful), it would have been very hard on her.

Little did we know what would come next.

During all of the commotion, I was talking to Mom about Natania's symptoms. She asked if Natania had a sore throat. I told her not really, but Natania did mention her throat hurt a little the night before. Mom mentioned I should consider taking her into the doctor for a strep test, just in case.

With Natania's heart-health history and surgeries, one of her greatest medical concerns was developing an infection—particularly through a strep infection. The reason for the concern is that the infection could settle in her heart since there is foreign substance there. She'd never had it before, but we've always been concerned about it. I try hard not to worry about it all the time, but every time she has a sore throat, I always monitor her closely.

This time she tested positive.

Had we been in Mexico, I would not have been talking to Mom; I would not have thought to take her to the doctor/hospital. Had we been to Mexico, I would have simply thought she was going through a stomach virus, and we would have likely been stuck in our hotel room the entire time. The real damage with strep comes when the person is not diagnosed and treated promptly. If someone in her condition was not properly treated, it could become a life-threatening situation within a couple of weeks.

If that was not enough, Natania also came down with a respiratory infection that piggybacked her strep infection. The treatment of her strep with a strong antibiotic was just enough to try to stay ahead of her getting full-blown pneumonia. If we had been in Mexico, she would not have been on an antibiotic, and we would not have had access to her nebulizer and Albuterol medication or inhaled steroid medication. Since we were still in town, we managed to stay *just* ahead of it all. We were trying to manage round-the-clock medication to keep her out of the hospital. I was concerned that because she was so ill she might not be able to attend the funeral. Luckily, she stayed just above the line and made it through.

I cannot begin to explain my feelings about the timing of Dean's death and Natania's situation. I felt in my heart that Dean somehow sacrificed himself for her.

The first few days after Dean died were a blur. I stayed up late, reading, drinking a glass or two of wine, and stopping every so often to sob. The first few nights I waited until the kids and Tim went to bed. I plopped into the couch and couldn't move. I sobbed and fell asleep and prayed and fell asleep and finally went up to bed at around 1:00 a.m. I knew it was a bad pattern to get into, but it was like it was my time to just think about Dean. It was such a shock. Dean always had a comforting presence about him, and now he was gone.

In addition to Dean's death and how the timing may have saved Natania, there was another miracle that happened with all of this.

My father, too, stayed up late at night, sometimes waking in the middle of the night, heartbroken over the loss of his only son. Several times, strange things happened to him in the midst of it all. First, you must know that my father has always been a bit of a skeptic about things. Early in my book, I gave a little background on this. He believes in God, but he still has questions about it. He struggles, as many do, when it comes to faith.

One day, just a few days after Dean died, Dad shared through his tears, "Dean was with me." For my father, this is not something he would make up. He's a "show me the evidence" kind of guy. If he didn't see or experience something first hand, he would not believe it. He woke up in the middle of the night, not being able to sleep, and went to the living room to sit in his Lazy-Boy type rocking chair. He was dozing in and out, when suddenly he felt something tugging on the blanket he was sitting on. He said it kind of scared him a little, because he knew someone was there, but when he looked, there was no one there. But the tugging continued, and Dad said he knew it was Dean. He also felt a sense of overwhelming peace surround him.

I must remind you again that never in a million years would my father admit to anything remotely "out there." For him to have experienced it and then shared it with others was a miracle. He told Mom right away, and based on everything that has happened in my life, he was anxious to share it with me.

A couple of days later, Dad experienced another life-altering experience. It was in the middle of the day. He was dozing off and on, when suddenly he saw the wall appear to open up like a vault door. An amazing light was behind the door as it opened. It was an extremely bright light. Someone came through the door and held the door open for another person, who walked out the door. Dad said the light that shown through was beyond words. The next person to come through was Dean. Dad said the amazing part was also how Dean's face was not shadowed. Dad went on to explain, "You know how if the sun or light is shining from behind someone, that person would be shadowed? Well, Dean's face was all lit up, as if the light was radiating from inside of him." He then went on to share that Dean did not have glasses on; he looked like he was in total happiness, contentment, and peace. He looked at Dad with the brightest smile he's ever seen and then . . . he gave Dad the "thumbs up." This is significant because that was a signal Dean used all the time, from when he was a small boy up until prior to his death. This time, however, Dean's arm was lifted high in the air, with his thumb up and a wide smile on his face.

Dad broke into tears several times as he tried to share the story with me. I know it was real, and I know it affected Dad in a way that is hard to put into words. I am so happy my father experienced this. I told Dad that I believed it was true, that Dean wanted Dad to know he was happy and was in heaven.

Mom and I were a little jealous that we didn't "see" Dean, although we quickly realized that it was Dad who needed to witness it first hand. If Dean appeared to Mom or me, Dad still would not have "gotten it." Dad was the one who needed this. Mom and I would believe through him, but it would not have happened if it was the other way around. I also feel this experience helped Dad with his faith. I am completely convinced Dean wanted to be sure we all would join him in heaven some day, and he knew Dad needed a little "evidence" to help him along.

Dean always worried fiercely about Mom and Dad. It is just like him to want to take care of them, to see them happy and safe. One advantage to his early death is that he will never have to worry about my mother or father passing before him. Most of our adult lives involved periodic discussions about Dad's health. Dad has always been quite healthy, although he's had some high blood pressure issues over the years. With our dad's own father dying fairly young of a sudden heart attack, it was always in the back of our minds (my father included). In fact, prior to Dean's death, Dean and I had another discussion about Dad's health when he was recently hospitalized at the same time as Dean after he collapsed at a wedding reception. It was after Dean was re-admitted to the hospital for his congestive heart failure, and Mom and Dad decided Dean was in good hands, so they could attend the wedding. They had planned to go to the wedding, visit Dean in the hospital, and then head to the reception.

It was good for Mom and Dad to get out and enjoy themselves after worrying about my brother for so long. Apparently Dad had been in a crowded, smoky bar area and started feeling light-headed and passed out. He hit the back of his head hard as he fell backward. My mom had just left to get him some ice when he initially started to feel light-headed. She was heading back to him when she saw him on the floor, surrounded by several people. Just to be safe, someone called 911 so Dad could be taken in for observation. Poor Mom! Dean was in one hospital, and now Dad was in another. That night (prior to learning about Dad), I had called Dean to see how he was doing, and he was concerned that Mom and Dad had not come back to see him yet. I remember reassuring him, saying Mom and Dad were probably just having a good time. A few minutes later, Mom called to tell me about Dad. My mom is the strongest woman I know, but I could tell she was really going through a lot. She tried to reassure me that she was fine. She was on a mission to take care of her men.

Both Dad and Dean would likely be discharged the next day, and Mom was trying to figure out how to juggle it all. I offered to pick up one or the other and to do whatever was needed, but she insisted on taking care of it. She planned to pick up Dad first and let him stay in the car while she went into the other hospital to get Dean. She wanted to be the one to talk to the doctors, so she could continue to be in control of their care when they got home.

When Dean and I spoke of Dad's visit to the ER, I could sense Dean's great concern. I could feel his worry. It was as if Dean was holding his breath.

Now, instead of Dean needing to worry about us and feeling like he had no control, he had that worry taken away and instead could make a difference in heaven.

This brings me to another experience my Dad had regarding Dean, and this time, it was in a dream. It was comforting and thought-provoking. Although Dean lived his life on Earth with disabilities, he doesn't have any in heaven, and while his true spirit always shined on others, he has nothing to hold him back anymore. In his dream, Dad was getting something out of an oven, and it was very heavy. He was about to drop it, when someone caught it. Dad turned around to thank the person, and it was Dean. Dad said, "Dean, I thought you were dead!" Dean said, "I am, but now I'm able to do things like this." It was as if he was communicating to Dad that he would always be there for us. He would be our guardian angel.

Once, not too long ago, I finally had a dream about Dean. In the dream, I cried and hugged him when I saw him and told him how much I missed him. He had no disabilities, and he was comforting me in such a wise way. While I sensed there might be danger or something bad about to happen, it was as if he wanted me not to worry—everything would be OK. It was as if he was willing to sacrifice himself again for me or my family, as if there would never be a question of this. I feel very blessed and humbled in this knowledge.

Regarding the visitation and funeral—it was a blur. We had to get there early, and many of those in our family were there. The saddest part of all was the fact that the entire extended family was all together, but Dean was not there to enjoy it—at least not in body. Since Dean's greatest joy was being in the presence of loved ones, the gathering was just not right.

The anticipation of seeing everyone the first time after Dean's death was hard. We all had a special connection with Dean. I know everyone worried about my parents. This was their *son*. They were supposed to have gone before him. A huge part of their life was taken away. While everyone tried to remember that Dean was in a better place, it was still hard to swallow.

I felt a special, different concern that our family and friends felt for me. They knew of Dean's and my relationship. They knew it was special. I still hate that Dean is not here (the child in me), but the wise, spiritual part of me is happy for him.

While we were children, I never wanted to be away from Dean. I still remember when we were little; Dean had to go into the hospital for an appendectomy. I missed him so much. Dean wasn't there, and it was not supposed to be that way. I remember crying for him. My parents said he'd be home soon. When he finally came home, I remember my parents first telling me they didn't know when he'd return from the hospital, but then they surprised me by saying someone was here—it was Dean! I remember carefully hugging him and being so happy to have him home.

Part of me feels like that little girl again. Dean and I were a team. Dean and Diane. Although I'm an adult now and have my own partner/husband, Dean was my first partner. Dean and I sat in the back of our parents' pick-up truck, holding a plastic garbage can full of fish from a fish hatchery. Dad was attempting to put them into the man-made pond at my parents' cabin. Dean and I went through chicken pox together. He got them first. While I was sad that I got them, I secretly felt it was cool to be like my big brother. It was Dean and I who sat in the back seat of our station wagon poking each other. Dad would say, "Fold your hands!" and then we'd elbow each other. But usually in car rides I'd sleep and Dean would stay awake so he wouldn't miss a thing. Dean was the one who hoped his baby sister would have a baby of her own to love, and who cried when he met his nieces for the first time.

Dean's wake was amazing. There was a stream of people coming to pay their respects. Even Jennifer's parents, Terry and Jackie Wing, came. They came to support me and to represent Jennifer. When I saw them, I ran to them and hugged them, with tears in my eyes. They had experienced a lot of health issues and miracles over the years themselves, and their presence meant so much to me.

Dean lived in Fort Atkinson, Wisconsin. I always worried about Dean and wanted to be sure he was safe and happy. When he moved out on his own, I never really knew much about his life. Sure, he told me how great everyone was. Most of them anyway.

There were a couple of times I heard about the "others." People who thought it was OK to bully or be mean to my brother. When we were young, some kids called him a "retard." Others pushed him around or laughed at him. In my mind, anyone who picked on someone like my brother was no more than a heathen. I turned into the strongest, loudest, scariest person when anyone hurt or was mean to my brother. Some bullies pushed his glasses off his face and shoved his books out of his arms. It broke my heart. He wouldn't hurt a fly, but some kids liked to use him as the target of mean jokes.

There was once a girl who lived on the way home from school, who did something I will never forget. Dean and I would walk home from school together, but sometimes we walked with our friends and apart from each other. His friend Todd would walk home with Dean. This particular day, Todd was not there. This girl was walking home from school too, but she was way ahead of me, closer to Dean. She started teasing him in a nasty way and proceeded to push him around a bit. She pushed his papers and books out of his arms. The papers flew all over the place. She also knocked his glasses off.

I remember being filled with rage for how hateful she was. I ran as fast as I could and screamed at her, pointing my finger in her face and maybe even grabbing her by her shirt. "You better pick up every one of Dean's papers right now, or I'll bash your face in!" I said. No one messes with me when I look them in the eye like that (or at least I like to think this). The girl looked at me like she believed me and proceeded to pick up all of the papers. I hope that in the years that have gone by, she has felt bad for what she did as a kid.

Another time, when Dean and I were in high school, he had a crush on a cheerleader from a different school. He was smitten by her, although I knew she was not genuine. The next year, I was cheerleading, and I overheard this girl telling some of the other cheerleaders about Dean—how he was a "retard," and teasing him behind his back. While I knew she was not the type of girl who could like my brother in that way, she was cruel in how she handled the situation. I happened to be standing there with all of the girls, and I stated loudly, "That guy happens to be my *brother*!" If looks could kill, I think I had daggers coming out of my eyes. She turned beet red. I walked away.

When Dean became an adult, he spent a short time in a group-home environment. We learned fairly quickly that it all was not as it was chalked up to be. While there were many good things about the group home, we also learned how many of the developmentally challenged people can become victimized. I am grateful my parents taught Dean right from wrong, something that I've found is not always the case with developmentally disabled individuals. Some are forgotten about or seen as a hindrance, or it is assumed they don't understand. Because my brother was raised with morals and values, he was better equipped to handle a frightening situation when a group-home manager made inappropriate advances to Dean. I am grateful Dean stayed away from him and told my parents and the police. He knew what the man was doing was not right. The man was used to getting away with it, but when he went after my brother, he got what he deserved. I was so proud of Dean.

Dean always had a hard time dealing with conflict or if he had done something he shouldn't have. Typically he would show signs of being upset in the way he acted. He would be distracted and quiet and look like the cat that ate the canary. He is like me in that regard: we couldn't hide anything.

When Dean was a bit older, he moved to Fort Atkinson. Most of the time, things were fine. One time I learned (after the fact) that he had been approached by a "gang." They told him to give them his money. He gave it to them, but they shoved him to the ground and kicked him more than once in the process. Thinking about this makes me so angry. I wished I could have been there to protect him. I think my adrenaline would have given me the strength of ten men, and I would have beaten them all with my bare hands. Hearing about this broke my heart.

Please remember the challenges faced by people with disabilities. Reach out and show kindness and love. If you ever witness cruelty like this, please have the courage to help the person. In honor of my brother, please don't ever forget.

Another time, Dean was at the local McDonalds. He went there often and always enjoyed going up to the counter to visit with the workers. Often he brought his heavy equipment magazines and brochures with him. One day, as he was talking to the workers, some teenage girls grabbed his magazines and brochures and ripped them up. Dean was very disappointed and told me what happened. He asked, "Why would they do that?" I told him we should feel sorry for those girls for being so bad that they think they need to do something like that. I said, "Just think about how shallow and empty they are to have done this." I told him not even to worry about stupid people like that. He seemed to think that made sense. What I really wanted to do was hurt those girls the way they had hurt my sweet brother. Dean seemed to forgive them, and instead, he let himself grow stronger as a result.

While Dean would tell me of the many friends he had in Fort, I was skeptical. I certainly wanted that for him—more than anything—but I didn't know if the people were genuine.

Another thing I miss are the calls from Dean. Even now, when the phone rings, for a split second I think it is Dean. Oh, how I miss that! He liked to call to share something exciting, like a good football game, or to announce something fun he had planned. He was always excited about simple things; he enjoyed life with a child-like perspective. He enjoyed what really matters.

When we planned the funeral, the last thing anyone expected was when my parents asked if I'd like to give a tribute or eulogy for Dean. As soon as it was suggested, I knew it was something I wanted and had to do—for Dean. For my beloved brother. I had to do something to give credit to his life and what he meant. I wanted everyone to know who Dean was and didn't want anyone to forget him. I wanted everyone to know how special my big brother was. Yes, I'm still grieving.

Why is it that it's only *after* someone is gone that we realize how much he/she meant to us? Why do we suddenly look at the person differently? Why do we only remember what really matters? Shouldn't every single day be spent like it is our last? Why don't we take the time to really get to know each other and understand each other? Why don't we ask all of those questions we might otherwise wonder about when they are gone? Why does life seem to keep going, even when you are not ready to move on?

As I worked on my eulogy for the funeral, I knew it had to be good. It was for Dean. When I sat down to type my eulogy, I said a prayer and asked God to guide me in the words I was about to type. The words seemed to flow perfectly.

When I was preparing to speak in front of everyone, I again said a prayer for God to help me deliver my message in the best way possible. It flowed just right. I'd like to share it with you:

"My brother, Dean"

DEAN'S EULOGY

What can I possibly say to accurately sum up Dean's life? Dean was . . . well, Dean. He was a smiling face with a twinkle in his eye. He so warmly and lovingly greeted all of us as if he was genuinely happy to see us. And he was.

Dean was the type of person who was real in everything he did. He was real in his love for others. He loved us all and saw the best in each of us and never spoke ill of anyone. Dean had a very loving and happy life, thanks to our parents, family, and friends. But he also experienced more than his share of challenges. Even when confronted with people who treated him badly through their ignorance, he never sought revenge (although I was not always so forgiving). He simply could not understand why people would be that way. When someone does not have a mean bone in his body himself, that makes sense.

Growing up, Dean and I shared a very special relationship. He always made me feel so loved. While many times I questioned the fairness of our differences, he only ever looked to me with genuine pride. He never seemed to think about himself or his own limitations, but instead was genuinely happy for others' accomplishments.

This was my brother, and he was such a blessing. He was the best. We always watched out for each other, and we looked up to each other. I remember when we were kids and he took it upon himself to prepare us some toast with peanut butter on it. He went about it in such a "big brother" way—taking care of his little sister and making sure she had breakfast. He even used a knife! (I think Mom and Dad were busy at the time.) I looked at him in awe and thought, "That is my brother."

Although I was three and a half years younger than he was, I was always fiercely protective of Dean. People usually saw me as a sweet little girl, but if someone was mean to Dean, I'd get right in their face and threaten them with their life (practically)! They didn't want to mess with me, even though I was half their size.

Dean knew better than most what life was really all about. He was wise in the way that really mattered. I love the story my mom once shared. Mom experienced blood clots in her legs after both Dean and I were delivered. It was important for her to try to keep her legs elevated whenever possible. After I was born, she would lie down to rest when I napped, and Dean would do the same. Dean was only three at the time, and he woke up from his nap early. Any typical three-year-old would have thought of himself and would have demanded attention. Not Dean. He saw Mommy was still napping, so he simply when back to his room to lie back down. That was Dean.

Another time, I remember visiting him at a group home he lived in when I was in college. My roommate was with me, and she acted very (regrettably) inappropriately when she was introduced to some people living with him. Dean matter-of-factly handled the situation in such a wise, mature manner by helping a person he lived with. He separated him from the situation in an attempt to spare his feelings. I again found myself looking at my brother in awe. That time he did, however, look at my roommate with disapproval. He never said another word about it, though.

Dean loved his truck magazines and books. Dean also so loved gatherings with his family and friends. One of my fondest memories of our adult life was when Tim and I planned a surprise 40th birthday party for him at our home. He loved every minute of it. We combined it with his dear cousin Iileen's baby shower, and we told each the party was a surprise for the other. Dean and Iileen didn't mind sharing the limelight with each other. Going back to his love of truck magazines and books . . . After the opening of the gifts came to a close, Dean was found outside (where it was quiet), reading a wonderful book he'd received from Iileen and her husband, David. Dean was on top of the world that day and so appreciated those who traveled to celebrate what meant so much to him.

Dean also loved his almanac and the Guinness Book of World Records. When he was not telling a joke, he'd be sharing an impressive fact he'd read with others. Sure, sometimes he'd interrupt, but he always offered some often-needed comic relief. Those who went to school with him shared with me that Dean always had a way of making them smile—who couldn't when they'd look at his sweet, innocent face?

Dean was such a proud and loving uncle to his four nieces. Dean knew it took extra prayers for Tim and me to finally become parents. I asked him to pray for us, and when we finally announced we were pregnant, he buried his head in his hands and cried. I will never forget when he came to visit Kianna after her birth. We walked together to her bassinet and cried together in joy. Dean was so proud upon the birth of all of the girls, and we have special pictures of him holding each one for the first time. This past summer, I was also grateful to Mom for bringing Dean to one of Kianna's soccer games. It was so great to have Kianna's godfather be included in part of our busy everyday lives.

We all have so many special memories: Dean's excited anticipation of Mom's wonderful meals, particularly as an adult; going to church with Mom and Dad, Tim, the girls, and me for the Christmas Eve candle-light service; and the excitement of almost starting one of the twins' hair on fire; and the time Tim took Dean to the UW Hockey game and Dean tried to learn what "sieve" meant, and finally, by the end of the game, learned the proper time to yell it. As a child, Dean thoroughly enjoyed spending a summer with Uncle Jim, Aunt Carol, Brian, Lisa, and Lori. He was treated with such love and respect by all of them, as well as by the entire little league team Jim coached.

Dean had the utmost respect for our parents. They loved him and helped him to realize the independence Dean craved. Thanks, Mom and Dad for caring and guiding Dean in such an admirable way. He knew how much you loved him. I am also so grateful to Mike and Claire for being there for Dean—taking him to dinner and to outings. Claire, I will forever be grateful that despite Mike's passing, you still selflessly continued to spend time with Dean—most importantly, taking him to the circus to help make his last day ideal.

Dean could not have accomplished what he did in his life without the help of special people from Opportunities. He was supported by his loving caseworkers—most recently, Rhonda. We all appreciate the friendship and help from Jackie. Those of us who lived with him knew he was not the tidiest person, but Jackie filled that gap so Dean could remain independent and live on his own. We all just wanted him to be happy. After meeting so many of his loving friends last night (at the wake), I can see we never had to worry about that.

With Dean's recent diagnosis of cardiomyopathy, it was becoming more challenging for Dean to remain independent while managing what he needed to do to care for himself. Although Mom and Dad continuously offered for him to stay with them, he insisted on getting back to his apartment. As much as he loved my family, the noise level in our house would have been unnerving for him. In either place, he would have been out of his comfort zone and away from everything he knew. When Mom asked Dean if there was anything they could do to make it easier for him, God answered for him and decided to take him home.

Dean deserves the best, and we are grateful God stepped in and is now caring for Dean. Mom and Dad had Dean in their care for forty-two years, and the time came for them to release him back into God's loving care. In heaven, Dean is now 100%. He has no more worries about what time to take his medication, when to get to his cardiac rehab appointments, how much exercise he was getting, recording his weight, what to eat, or worry about making sure he didn't take in more than a certain amount of fluids each day. Dean no longer has to worry about Mom and Dad—always concerned about the future. Dean can finally be at complete peace in heaven. We can be comforted, knowing Dean is with Grandma Thorpe and Grandpa, and Grandma and Grandpa Tousignant. And Aunt Carol and Uncle Mike and Andrew and Mary. He is probably up in heaven right now teaching little James some jokes or Crazy 8's. Dean is experiencing peace and joy beyond our understanding, and no one deserves this more than my dear brother.

We can learn a lot from Dean. There are so many things we worry about and focus on that do not matter. Each of us can remember the light that shone through Dean that was passed on to others. If we can all remember the importance of treating each other with love and kindness above all else, we too, can rest in peace, knowing we left this world a better place.

In the beginning, and throughout my eulogy, at Tim's suggestion, I incorporated "Dean-type" jokes. Like knock-knock jokes. This seemed fitting, and I think it was appreciated by everyone in the room. It sure helped break up the seriousness of it all. When the tone of my eulogy turned sullen, I would interject with another joke.

Saying goodbye to my brother was like a part of me being left behind. I can only imagine how my parents felt. Just like when we were kids and he had his appendix out, I didn't want him to be away from me. I didn't want to leave him.

I was grateful to the many people who came to show their respects. My dear mother and father-in-law, two sisters-in-law, Melanie and Chrissy, and two nieces, Angela and Alison, all came to be there for us. Our dear friends Kevin and Melissa took the day off from work to be there. My friends Jody, Annie, Sara, Kathy, and so many others all came to support me and my family. Even one of the "bullies" I spoke of earlier came. While he could not stay, he looked me in the eye with great sincerity. Dean never held the past against this person but instead befriended him. I could see in this person's eyes that he genuinely cared for Dean.

People from Tim's office, whom my parents and I were meeting with to plan my parents' will in relationship to how Dean would be cared for, even attended. One of the founding partners of Tim's company also came to pay his respects the night of the visitation. While they had not met Dean, I think they heard enough about him through my parents and me. During the last meeting with them, in fact, we were discussing Dean's future, and I broke down in the meeting as I shared my concern over his happiness and safety. In discussing details of their will, I stated how I wanted Dean to live closer to me, so I could be there for him. It meant a lot to us that they took time from their busy days to offer their sympathy.

I learned more about Dean's adult life *after* his death, more than I ever imagined. As I mentioned in the eulogy, Dean was well cared for in Fort Atkinson. We received such an outpouring of support from so many people through cards, flowers, and gifts. I was always suspicious of the people Dean talked about, but after meeting them in person, I saw that they were good people—good people who did not have developmental issues themselves, but who took Dean under their wing and loved him. I saw in their tearful eyes that they had lost their best friend. I never had any reason to doubt their sincerity. To Dean's friends Don and Scott, and so many others, I thank you from the bottom of my heart.

The town of Fort Atkinson, Opportunities Inc., and the Parks and Recreation department all coordinated a party to honor Dean a few weeks after his death. Mom and Dad were presented with an award celebrating

Dean's Special Achievements in his life from the State Representative, Andy Jorgensen. Many people came to show their respects. There was a DJ who invited anyone to come forward and share a story about Dean or tell jokes. The room was filled with very special people, all of whom loved my brother. It is hard to explain, but I felt like I was able to see into the souls of these special people. I looked beyond their disabilities and saw into their hearts. I realized how, like Dean, they "get life" in a way most of us do not. They don't judge people the way most do. They seem to look into the hearts of others. As I saw everyone dancing, some "fast" dancing, some who liked to dance like Elvis, and some who danced slowly as they held each other close, I realized how simple life should be. It's about being there for each other and being kind to one another. It's about offering support and love.

There was one special lady there. At first I was not sure if she had some developmental challenges herself, or was a volunteer, but she seemed very broken up about Dean's passing. Maybe more so than the others. She was in charge of asking everyone to comment about Dean in a book she put together. I came up to her and could tell she is a very caring person. She tearfully shared with me that she had to "step in to take over where Dean left off." That made me cry all over again.

If more people would take the time to get to know people who are different from them, whether it be someone with disabilities or someone who has a different view of life, different beliefs, different race or social status, they may learn something. Having an open mind and a new perspective of what makes everyone unique can make a significant difference in our lives. God wants this. Our main purpose in life is to love one another. While we each may have our own specific role, when combined, we offer the perfect balance. All we need is to love and respect each other's unique differences.

So why this final chapter and all of the details? Well, part of it is just a way for me to get over the loss of Dean. It is fresh in my mind, and I needed to get it out. Adding this final chapter, while unexpected, has also been a way for me to offer another perspective and story of life, the challenges we face, and God's role within it. And finally, it is a way to honor the perspective of Dean. One who saw the best in everyone he met. One who didn't see disabilities in himself or in others. He loved people for who they are, the way God wants us to. Dean approached life by accepting the challenges and difficulties the way God would have wanted us to—with his famous "thumbs up."

As I'm putting the final touches on my book—this time, I am not waiting for any other chapters to be added—it's October 11, 2007. The clock on the laptop reads 10:51 p.m. We are getting by. The loss of Dean is still very hard, and we are still healing. Nothing will ever fill the void, but we have been able to see, once again, how God works in our lives.

Sometimes life can be sad and scary, but even greater, there is joy and happiness. It depends on where you look. Asking God into your heart will help you to be fulfilled and enable you to complete your own "Full Circle" of life and love. Again I say . . . may God be with you.

Answered Prayer

I asked God for strength, that I might achieve,
I was made weak, that I might learn humbly to obey.

I asked for health, that I might do greater things,
I was given infirmity, that I might do better things.

I asked for riches, that I might be happy,
I was given poverty, that I might be wise.
I asked for power, that I might have the praise of men,
I was given weakness, that I might feel the need of God.

I asked for all things, that I might enjoy life,
I was given life, that I might enjoy all things.

I got nothing that I asked for—
But everything I had hoped for;

Almost despite myself,
My unanswered prayers were answered.
I am among all men most richly blessed.

—*Unknown Confederate Soldier*

LaVergne, TN USA
25 March 2010
177145LV00001B/5/P